SALES GENIE

RETAIL MARKETING 101

5 EFFECTIVE WAYS TO INCREASE RETAIL SALES

& BOOST PROFIT BY

25% IN 60 DAYS

BY

Shabbir Hossain

Copyrights

Copyright (C) 2016 CSB Academy Publishing Co.

CSB Academy Publishing Co.

P. O. Box 966
Semmes, Alabama 36575, USA
Design & Layout
By
Rita Hossain
First Edition

Edited by Juliann Barnhard

INTRODUCTION

After writing my very first book on How to Stat, Run and Grow a Successful Gas Station Business, I thought I was done with writing for good. But lately, I have been getting a lot of email questions and concerns from my podcast listeners and from the book and Blog readers about the issues they are facing in their business. Most of which I can summarize in three categories.

- ➢ Lack of sales volume

- ➢ Lack of profitability

- ➢ Operational challenges and issues

As I reply to them (I try my best to reply to as many as I possibly can), I kept thinking why don't I summarize some of these issues and remedies in a book and offer it to my readers and listeners.

As of now, my main business is Gas Station/Convenience stores. But in the last 25 plus years, I have owned, managed, and or operated a few other types of retail businesses like fast food franchises, Italian restaurant, pizza delivery business, dry cleaner, B2B wholesaling, and even liquor stores.

At one point, a large oil company offered me a deal where I would take over their underperforming locations and make them profitable in less than six months so they can sell or lease those locations at a better price. I was being compensated very well, but the sacrifice I was making in my personal life was enormous. After doing it for a few years, I decided to quit as I was facing the same issues in my own businesses.

Since I was always on the road working for the oil company, my own businesses were being negatively affected. I was seeing the sales declining, and so were the profit, and at one point I was pouring money that I was making at my job into my business. A truly counterproductive situation right?

I thought so too, so I ended the contract and came back to focus on my own businesses. But during the time I was working with the oil company, I was able to turn nine businesses around. The sales increased from 20% to as high as 60% in some stores. I mastered a simple yet proven method that I created to improve those businesses. Don't get me wrong, in turn; I made great money. But this is not about me; it's about you and your business. So let's talk about it.

Anyone who owns a retail business knows how tough it can be to navigate the business environment. Bigger sales volume is any store's prime objective. After all, that is what will contribute to increased profits and business growth. However, if you have tried doing that, you know it is not an easy task. There are many aspects and angles, which you can take to look at a problem and retail sales are one such issue that requires multiple efforts. There is no simple formula for it or a rule that you could follow to get ahead of your competitors. It requires keen observation of your business operations and consistent efforts to continue to grow.

First, you have to take a bird's eye view of your business, identify the issues you are facing, make a note of why you think you are losing sales or your sales volume is not where it should be. Ever met a business broker when they are showing you a business for sale? They will often tell you the sales volume and then give you a laundry list of things that you can do as the new owner to improve sales. Well sometimes that is what you need, an outsider looking at your business with some business commons sense to tell you what you need to do to improve your business.

The retail industry is considered an indicator of economic progress as retail sales account for almost two-thirds of the US Gross Domestic Product. It is also a very competitive process as every penny counts. You simply cannot afford to believe that opening a store is all that you need to do to kick-start sales. You may have a physical presence, great products, and a warm environment, but still, if you see that your customers aren't turning into clients, then there is something missing.

In this book, I try to break down the anatomy of retail sales for you and look at five productive ways that you can increase your sales and boost profits. After all, the more sales your business can make, the more profitable it will be for you right? I tried to bring you the true, tested, and proven methods that can increase sales, and if you remain consistent in your efforts, you can *improve your sales by 25% in only 60 days*. Now that is something! At a glance, you will find:

> - Identifying the true issues
> - The current challenges and solutions
> - 5 Proven ways to boost sales
> - 4 Steps to reach 25% sales increase in 60 days
> - The future of retail business

One more thing I need to mention before we start. I know I may not be able to answer or satisfy every reader's mind, if you don't find the answers you are looking for in this book, my humble request is that you contact me, and if it is within my knowledge and power I will try my best to help you find the answer.

You can find me in few ways, first, stop by my blog at GasStationBusiness101.com and you can contact me from there. You can also find me on Facebook at CSB_Academy. You can also email me directly at shabbir@gasstationbusiness101.com and send me your questions. If you enjoy listening to the audio podcast, you can listen to my Gas Station Business 101 Podcast show on iTunes, Stitcher or TuneIn Radio.

Okay, time to get started, so let's begin!

9 KNOWN PROBLEMS WITH RETAIL SALES

To understand retail sales, you have to recognize the problems first. All business owners know how important it is to increase sales, and I am sure most of you do want to increase sales. But why do you then still fail to achieve the sales target?

What is it that differentiates your business from your competitor who is essentially selling the same merchandise? Surely, there are many factors involved but let's take a look at some of the problems that may be affecting your retail sales. Keep in mind that all of these may not apply to your business, but it is a good idea to keep a note of the ones that you think do affect your business. Ready? Let's dive in.

NEGLECT

Setting up any business requires a visionary entrepreneur, but forming a company is only part of the challenge and the rest lies in continuous and consistent direction and involvement from the leadership. Without that, a company can soon lose its direction and fail to sustain itself in the face of new problems and challenges. For a company to boost its sales, it's important to continuously review, maintain, and develop it to keep it at its peak performance.

At no point can a company be neglected and still hope to run profitably. External forces that affect a company's bottom line are forever changing, and any neglect can throw a retail sales business off spin. As an owner, whether it's a small shop, big boutique, or a gas station, you need to take notice of the changing factors and change along with them to keep the business up to date and to thrive.

TUNNEL VISION

When you work IN your business every day, it is hard to look at it from a distance and analyze problems. Essentially, that is what we call tunnel vision. You are so consumed in your everyday operation that you can't figure out what it is that you or your employees are doing wrong, or not doing at all.

Remember, the business broker example I just mentioned, well you need an outside perspective in your business. It also helps to ask your customers what they want to see in your business or what areas need improvement. Listen to them and write it down.

CASH FLOW ISSUE

Cash is King! Cash is also an important part of your business growth, and while a company may have started with a minimum of financial capital, there may reach a point when additional money is required to grow or to buy additional inventory or to do some much-needed upgrades. If additional funds are not available, it could be difficult for a business to meet its day to day obligations which can hamper your ability to increase sales.

Mastering the art of managing money is one of the key resources of a business that helps it keep within its limits and maximize the use of its available funds. Any company that goes over the limit in debt fails to see the light of day. Many small retail stores don't follow proper accounting practices which could be a big dent in their time and efforts around tax filing season or when they go to get a loan.

Having your business finances in order, whether yourself or through a professional accountant, ensures that you keep track of your money and understand how much the business is making in profits. Making projections for the future becomes easier when you have everything organized in accounting software and not on paper.

EVER INCREASING OVERHEAD COST

As important as it is to study success, the same is true of failure. It points out the glitches in the system, which can lead to success if they are overcome. No process is efficient from the beginning, but it is made so with continuous improvements and developments, which is all due to the effort of a business's leadership. When starting a new business, most people overlook failures and focus only on making money.

Money can be made only when you look at potential problems and know how to overcome them. Business growth is a learning process, but the better prepared you are, the farther you will go. As a business owner, your primary focus should be to efficiently run your business with the best resources available to you and make it a lean, mean machine so everyone knows the process and can repeat the same result every time. Money is a byproduct of success, so if you run your business effectively, the money will come. Sounds easy I know but it is not hard to do.

The retail sales industry is an evolving and rapidly changing industry with technology stepping in to shape the nature of things for good. How well you adapt to each coming change defines your ability to succeed in the retail world. Success and profits come only after you are able to provide your customer with a valuable experience.

Businesses that work on developing good customer experiences through their sales and after sale services and by making the process smooth find it easier to discover their path to growth. That's because your customer should be your priority and not your business because that's what makes your business a success. Considering them as an integral part of your business is what will allow you to continuously find and nurture new opportunities to provide a better experience.

With the rapid changes in the business world, the cost of doing business is going up too, and that is one uphill battle that is harder to win. From labor cost to utility bills, everything is going up. But your profit margin is not going up nor is your sales volume. Lately, some of us in retail are faced with the new cost of technology like EMV updates. Most cash registers and ATM machines are now required to be upgraded to handle the Chip-based credit cards. This is a huge upfront cost and in some businesses, it can cost as much as $20,000 to comply with the new guidelines.

LEADERSHIP ISSUES

Management problems are real issues, and they can destroy a company. While an entrepreneur may be effective at starting a business from a mere idea, they may not be ready to face the management problems associated with it. If you don't have good people on your team, if you don't train them properly, if you don't coach them often, if you don't pay them enough or aren't willing to treat people the right way, then chances are, your company will suffer. High turnover is a significant cost that a company faces if its employees frequently leave due to a toxic work environment.

Being an entrepreneur isn't only about setting up a business and growing it continuously to reach higher milestones. It's also about improving yourself, your skills, and knowledge. Collaboration and delegation are traits that every entrepreneur should master if they are to succeed.

One man alone can't do everything when things have been set in motion, and while you are taking care of the big things that affect a business directly, there are many smaller things that have an impact on a business indirectly.

Internal mayhem can easily be one of those hidden reasons for a company's failure and sometimes, the top leaders fail to see that. While the top leadership is busy articulating the company's future, its internal friction can lead to inefficiency, low motivation, and decreased productivity. In the retail sales industry, the employee turnover is usually high; this is mostly due to the internal inefficiency of the company.

CUSTOMER EXPERIENCE

Thirty percent of all new businesses fail in the first three years not because they didn't have great products, location, or pricing, but because they had bad customer service. Put yourself in your customer's shoes and see if you would like the same treatment and experience if you were the customer. If you know of any business that you often go to and love going there because of how they treat you, analyze why and what you like about them. See if you are offering the same experience to your customers. If not, why?

Apart from these, there can be many other problems that business owners' face. From the store outlook to its experience and staff management. There are all sorts of factors that affect retail sales no matter what kind of business you are running and to thrive it's important to be aware of them and work on correcting them. Retail store owners, for instance, are continually faced with the problem of enhancing their customer's store experience and navigation effectiveness. From the moment the customer walks into a store to the time they leave, everything needs to be accounted for. How the sales person greets and assists the customer and whether the products are on display in the most productive way are major concerns for any retail store.

Hiring sales staff that is alike is another problem in retail stores because it limits growth potential. Your customers aren't all alike when it comes to their likes and dislikes, and it's important to have a diversified workforce to cater to all kinds of customers that walk in. Most patrons don't like being left alone in a store and want the staff at hand to help them navigate or find a particular item. All this relates to how you manage your sales personnel and how warmly they entertain the in-store customer.

Not only should your products be on display at the right places where you know your customers will be able to grab them effortlessly, thus increasing sales, but also, your store experience should uplift their shopping experience. Take for instance Apple's engaging in-store experience which apart from the products is a fun and exhilarating experience for customers.

Aesthetically pleasing designs and interactive displays are the heart of their store. While all stores don't have the resources to go to such lengths to make the in-store experience stand out, understanding that it is significant to draw the customer in.

There is always something that you can change to enhance your customer's in-store experience significantly. Every store must have a differentiation plan, and that is one of the things that most stores lack. Among many other businesses that are exactly like you, that pose competition to you, how do you stand apart from them?

This is another problem in retail sales business that owners need to sort out before they step into reap profits. This issue revolves around branding, but many companies learn that providing greater customer service can also help boost sales.

When you are in a highly competitive market, selling the exact same things as your competitor, what really differentiates you from them is any kind of superior customer service that you can offer. Whether it is home delivery, discounts, after sale product care, free returns or exchanges, online order placement, or faster query response. All these things go a long way in differentiating one retail unit from another.

OVEREXPANSION

I was guilty of this a few times myself, so I suppose I am the best one to talk about it. When I bought my first Quiznos fast food franchise, I was pleasantly surprised to see how simple yet manageable that business was, and how much money I was making. So in just two years I grew to five locations and then overexpansion hit me like a freight train. Over the next two years, for many reasons, some beyond my control, like the economic meltdown of 2008, I started to suffer financially, mentally, and even physically, as it was hard to manage and supervise all of them.

The lesson I learned was while growth is important for business, growing too quickly can also turn into a problem and disrupt the business process. When a company becomes too big without proper procedures in place or by defying the normal growth cycle, it can become difficult to handle. Problems in logistics, supply, financing and staffing start becoming apparent and the overexpansion, instead of being a step forward, turns into an obstacle in growth. Without a proper strategy and preparation, business growth can stifle the progress of any business, and soon, it may be striving for survival.

It's important for any retail sales business to grow steadily, to have a strategy in place and the right people to execute it. People can make all the difference when it comes to your business making it big or not. Eventually, it's the people who will be doing the work and executing the plan, so the more skilled, diversified, and integrated team that you have running your business, the better results it can help produce.

When hiring management or other staff, it is paramount for a company to hire people who are well aligned with its philosophy and goals. Every company has core values and a centralized philosophy that it stands for. Any misalignment in that and in between your employees will always cause friction and prevent smooth operations from making a foothold. Growth is welcome even at a fast pace, but if you don't have the capabilities and resources to handle it, you can find yourself in the midst of mayhem.

THEFT, FRAUD & OTHER CRIMES

It seems like theft and fraud are almost an inevitable part of the retail business. It is a reality, it is a fact, and it can be anyone, from your vendors to employees, customers, and partners. There is an absolute limit of due diligence that a company can perform, but beyond that, avoiding theft and fraud is unavoidable. The best plan of action against theft is to have proper policies and insurance in place to be ready for it if it happens.

You may not be able to stop 100% of the theft or fraud, but as long as you keep it to a minimum, consider yourself lucky. Remember, internal theft and fraud can cost you much more than most external ones. You should be careful and have a formal hiring process in place, which at least allows you to sift candidates based on education, experience, personality, and customer service skills. You can ask for a criminal background check and offer to pay for it.

Apart from the internal and external theft and fraud, there is one more thing we all have to worry about which is a crime against our businesses. Since we are in retail, we deal with cash and often times we are subject to robbery and break-ins. You should have a particular cash handling procedure in place, not more than $100 in any cash register at any given time. The rest has to be dropped into the safe.

Practice safety and coach your employees often, then come and spot check them to see if they are carrying more than $100 in their register at any time. Post a sign on your front door stating that you do not carry more than $100 in your register and that the cashier cannot open the safe. Most large retailers practice these safety procedures and you should too. I will discuss most of these in more detail in a later chapter.

COMPETITION

Last, but never the least, we need to talk about one of the biggest problems most of us face in our business - competition. It is the unhealthy competition that hurts us the most. When a big name retailer has a location near you, often times they try to undercut you in pricing to steal business from you. Though it is not illegal to do so, in my opinion, it is unethical. Often times they undercut prices where they sell below your cost and essentially force you to do the same.

The best way to battle this war is to win your customers and clients with an outstanding customer service experience. Wow them, bond with them, get to know them. A customer that you know by their first name will come back to your store over and over even if you are little higher on your prices compared to the big name retailers next door.

It is proven, give it a try. No, I am not asking you to increase your prices and charge more. But as long as you are competitive within reason, you can win them over with excellent customer service. People, in general, want that bonding, it is basic human nature.

5 CHALLENGES IN THE RETAIL INDUSTRY

When you look at the retail industry along with its obvious problems in today's world, there are solid challenges that need to be addressed if you are to move forward with it profitably. No business is devoid of challenges, and if you can overcome the following difficulties, you can be on your way to boosting sales.

How a business operates has changed significantly in the past few years. With newer technology and technological and cultural shifts taking place, there is no denying the fact that the environment has become competitive. While before, there may have been different kinds of challenges to deal with, now, the nature of challenges that retail businesses face has changed. The environment to conduct business hasn't remained as easy, and it's becoming difficult for retailers to boost their sales and profits.

However, if you are willing to adopt the new models and technologies in your retail business and use creative methods to attract customers, which aligns with their expectations, then you will be able to rise above the competition and boost your sales. This is crucial to understand in the retail business. The challenges it faces today will be entirely different in the next few years, and retailers who are not willing to take action now will be left far behind. To succeed, you have to think ahead five years and review your practices to align them with customer expectations.

The environment in which business is conducted today is a lot different from what it used to be. Whereas before, retailers had the power to influence a customer's decision, today, they don't. Power has significantly shifted to the consumer and if you're not willing to admit that and act accordingly, it will be the very first obstacle in your growth. Let's review the challenges currently facing the retail industry as a whole.

DATA MANAGEMENT

Data management is crucial in today's age. There is a large amount of data that is available to retailers today which is significant to drawing conclusions and solid evaluations. The challenge that the industry faces today is how to please the growing amount of consumer expectations because most customers now have access to a large amount of information, which puts them in a position to choose between one retailer or another.

If you're not acting upon data collection and management, you will be losing your customers. The key is to enhance the customer experience because with every retailer selling the same items, how will you set yourself apart from the others?

Retail businesses that focus on setting themselves apart will be able to stay a step ahead of their competitors as technology and innovation lead the way. Customers look for a smooth experience without any glitches and most want to be able to use their smartphones to make the purchases.

Take the example of a simple gas station business. Data can help it grow as it evolves into a touch point that attracts more customers and offers new services. How you understand your customer plays a vital role in how you are going to market your services to them. Data also affects the kinds of products that should be stocked on shelves of the convenience store to target its market and provide a unique customer shopping experience.

How data is collected, stored, and managed has a profound impact on how you are going to use it to increase sales and boost profits. In the future, a gas station is not going to remain a simple gas station, or it isn't, even now. With the introduction of technology, it will have evolved into a place that gives a superior customer experience to its target audience, which ranges from conventional customers to travelers and other groups that are looking for a place beyond a simple gas station.

MAKING PAYMENTS SAFE AND SECURE

Securing the Point of Sale and Customer data is another big challenge facing the retail industry and keeping the finance execs up at night. This is critical, because if you're not able to secure your POS system, it could lead to losing a customer's trust and eventually, the customer. Any customer that interacts with a retailer does so, on the condition of trust.

Some of the biggest retail chains also face the problem of securing their payment systems and making them safe.

Accidents can happen to anyone, and while you are taking action to prevent unsafe transactions, it is crucial to know how you are going to deal with a mishap. Most retailers do everything in their power to make their payment terminals safe and secure and advertise it as such. However, when something goes wrong, they are unable to deal with it.

In the event of a crisis, it is important to have a contingency plan to overcome the challenges of secure payments. While you can do everything to make it safe, what you do after an accident takes place is also important. How you handle your clients in the aftermath of an accident shows your worth as a retailer and how much you care about the customer.

Most retailers fail when it comes to owning their fault and standing up to their customers and apologizing. Another thing in making payments secure is the new technology and payment methods, making their way in. It will become increasingly difficult to make all the payment modes safe and secure.

Currency is increasingly becoming digital with Apple and Google paving their way into the market with digital payments. This makes it a big challenge for retailers too, on the one hand, become part of the movement while on the other, also partner up to make it safe for their customers.

In the retail world, I am sure most of you have noticed the new credits cards with the Chip in them. These are the steps all credit card and other companies are taking to battle the ever growing battle with fraud.

All the credit card companies together started a new and safer way to handle payments which is known as EMV (Europay, MasterCard, and Visa) update; this update requires all retailers to upgrade their POS hardware to be able to handle the new chip cards and to ensure safety for both the consumers and retailers.

CUSTOMER ACQUISITION

Customers are the heart of any retail business, and if you are not able to attract customers, you will not be able to make sales and thus, make a profit. A certain amount of customers may allow you to break even, but to enhance your profit margin; you need to keep attracting new customers. With the increasing competition, customer acquisition has also become difficult, and it has not remained as easy for retailers to acquire new customers.

What customers need is an enhanced shopping experience, and with the introduction of e-commerce, store sales are primarily getting affected, except for necessary commodities for which a customer has to step out. Evolving the customer experience is a crucial step forward to increase sales and acquire new customers.

For instance, take a gas station business, and you'll be quick to agree that it has evolved from a mere gas station to a mini grocery store. Customers not only go there to refill their gas tank but look forward to a customer experience that helps them relax and unwind. Even your average customer may like coming there often if you provide them with an all-around experience and fulfill their immediate needs.

How you enhance your customer's experience in any retail store has become extremely crucial to make them stay, return for another purchase at a later time, and spread the word about your business.

THE EVOLVING CUSTOMER PROFILE

Your average customer is not average any longer. With the flow of information and communication and how readily it has become available to customers today, there is a big challenge for retailers to overcome when it comes to influencing the customer to make a purchase at their store. Customers today are highly informed and have all the tools at their disposal to make their decision.

From pricing to product reviews, a customer knows how to navigate their way through the retail shopping experience, and they do not settle for anything less than they expect. The options that they have at their disposal are endless, so the best of retailers should be focused on making their user journey as smooth and positive as possible. You want them to be directed towards your product from among all the other options and end up purchasing it.

Be it any retail business; customers look forward to a smooth and satisfactory experience. They have high expectations when it comes to placing an order and expect fast customer service as well. Customers today are in such a hurry that they don't like to wait around. For this reason, retailers have to focus increasingly on making their experience speedy as well as comfortable.

EMPLOYEE EFFICIENCY

Your employee is your biggest asset because if they are going to greet and deal with the customer effectively, then the customer will feel engaged. It is a challenge for retailers to find and keep good employees and help them grow as well. Only a happy employee will make your customer happy which will result in helping maintain good relations with the customers and contributing to increased customers. More customers reflect on a business's bottom line, and that's what any retailer wants.

However, keeping all or most of the employees happy and utilizing their full potential is a big challenge and is easier said than done. Your employees come from all sorts of backgrounds, and you can only do so much to help them. Apart from the necessary facilities, which should be in top order to keep employees satisfied, a mix of other incentives, which motivate them, should help to keep them satisfied at their job.

Any retail business that hires employees also needs to make sure they are hiring the right candidate for the job. For this, you need to know the qualities that you are looking for in an employee when you're hiring because otherwise, you will remain unable to tackle the challenge, more on this in a later chapter so stay tuned.

THE 5 PROVEN WAYS TO INCREASE SALES

Any retailer that wants to survive the competitive environment and increase their sales needs to take into account their personal progress as well as their customer's sales experience. A well-managed and healthy business that grows in profits on a year-to-year basis is one which is well organized and well-coordinated. Business is like a machine, and if you're not going to keep it well oiled, it will one day stop working.

To boost your sales, you have to bear in mind that the most valuable asset of your company is its customers, and your sales should be increasing in such a way that it does not threaten or harm the customers. The minute your customer feels that your business is stepping over them to increase its sales; they can change their direction and go to a competitor. Be it a store, a gas station or other kind of retail business, your customer should always stay on top of the list.

Businesses often forget the power of the customer and in a competitive environment, how you deal with your customer is the most important thing. For any business to boost its sales, diversity is imperative among other things. How you set yourself apart from the pack is the factor to drive sales. However, for any retail business's success, there are two things which are critical.

Apart from the external forces affecting the business and how they are handled, a company needs to fine-tune its internal processes as well. If a retail business only considers responding to external changes and overlooks internal processes and change management, it cannot be efficient and will sooner or later face problems. On the other hand, an organization that only focuses on strengthening its internal processes but ignores the external shifts will again collapse as it will be unable to provide a unique experience in line with customer demands.

If you really want to boost your retail sales, you have to look at both things simultaneously and work on developing them. Sometimes, the answer lies in not the big things but in the small. Often the most overlooked areas of the business are those that are actually causing the loss and hold significance.

Any smart retailer knows not to underestimate any aspect of their business and work on all facets to make it profitable. Here are the five ways you can boost your retail sales and enjoy greater profits. I have been practicing these five elements in my business for many years so this is not just a theory, these are proven methods that are easy to follow.

Now, this is how I break down this process. First, let's talk about what you sell. The products, the merchandise or the services, and the pricing. Then we will touch on people or your workforce. Next, we will discuss how to market and promote your merchandise or product in the most productive way. Next, we will discuss how to minimize operating cost and make your business lean and mean which includes your buying process and from who, so it is all about vendor negotiation. Lastly, we will touch on how to minimize theft and errors in your business. Sounds good? Let's do this.

Oh one more thing, I just wanted to mention since for the most part, my background is in gas station, fast food franchise, liquor store type retail businesses, the real life examples I am using in this book will mostly be from those businesses, but this will not mean that the same methods can't be applied in most other retail businesses. So just try to imagine and modify (as you see fit) the methods to custom fit in your business.

1. PRODUCT MERCHANDISING & PRICING

First, let's define what a product is. For most retail businesses it is the merchandise that we carry in our stores. You may ask what is the big deal about products and merchandising when it comes to a small business since every store similar to yours carries the same products right?

Well, wrong! There's no "one size fits all" in this business. You have to differentiate your store/business from the next store to stand out in the crowd. Product selection is the differentiator that can make you a success as opposed to a not so good product selection that can tank your business into the ground.

So now the obvious question you will ask is what is a good product selection versus a bad product selection and how do you know which one is good when it comes to picking up the right product line for your business?

That is what we will be discussing. There are four very important things you need to find out about your store, about your customer base and the demographics of your store first, before you can decide what and how to merchandise your business with the right products.

1. The median income level of your customer base in the area (to detect if it is a blue or white collar area).

Knowing the income level of your customer base will give you an idea if you are in a blue or a white collar neighborhood. First, where do you find this information? The best place is the US census bureau, and you can do a search by zipcode. Just follow the link, and you will see the US Census site.

> https://www.census.gov/
> Or try
> https://www.census.gov/quickfacts/table

Once you know the average income level of your customer base, you can then figure out if your customer base is predominantly blue or white collar or if it is a mixed neighborhood. As I am sure you can understand, the buying behavior is very different between these two groups.

2. Race and ethnicity of the customer base. Yes, we will have to talk about the very sensitive issue of race here, I know but stay with me, and I will explain why.

Race can play a significant role in your merchandising effort for your store, and again I will explain more in detail later on. First, let me point you to where you can find that information for your area. Once again direct your browser to the US Census site and there you can find out this very vital piece of information as well.

3. Age of the population or your customer base.

Similarly, the age of the population plays a big role as far as their buying habits. Thus your merchandising effort too, and again you can find the median age of the population of your area from the same US Census site. Now gather up all this information, and we will talk about how to put them to good use.

4. Location of your store (is it in the city, inner city or in a rural area).

This 4th element is easy to figure out; you don't need to visit a website to know this. Just look around you. I am sure you already know if your store is in the city, inner city, or rural community.

Most successful retailers have similar market research methods that they practice as a part of their product selection strategy.

Now let me start by giving you some examples.

One prominent example is Wal-Mart. To give you a clear picture of how merchandising is done in big retail chain companies, let's take a look at three Wal-Marts; one in rural Mississippi, one is El Paso, TX, which is on the border of Mexico, and the last one is in China. Do you think every Wal-Mart carries the same product line in every store they operate? The answer is no. A Wal-Mart in China will carry vastly different products than the one say in Mississippi or Texas; I think we can agree on that.

Now let's talk about some of the differences between the store in rural Mississippi versus the one in El Paso, Texas. Once you browse the aisles of the El Paso store, you may notice products and foods are more Spanish influenced than the store in Mississippi. But why do you think they are so different? The answer is demographics. This is where the race, income level, and age come into play. But in this case, the race or ethnicity is the number one differentiator here.

There are more Spanish-speaking people in El Paso then there are around the store in Mississippi. When you walk down each shopping aisle in both of these stores, you will notice subtle differences, but not every product will be different, just a few in every aisle. For example, if you walk the milk and juice aisle, you may see rice milk alongside regular milk which you will not see in the Mississippi store. Walk the juice section you will see guava juice, mango juice, or tamarind juice next to orange juice in the El Paso store which you will not see in the store in Mississippi.

If you walk the fruits and vegetable aisle in the El Paso store, you may find fresh green coconut, a bigger selection of radish and cilantro compared to the store in Mississippi.

I hope you get my point. So as you can see, selecting the right products based on your immediate neighborhood clientele is the key to your success. Remember it is the products that you carry which attract people to your store. If a customer knows you carry a certain type of bread or tobacco that is not carried by your competitor, then yes, he or she will come to your store every day and shop with you.

When doing the layout of your store and product selection, you don't have to go item by item, but you have just to tweak a few notches to make it unique and appropriate for that exact neighborhood. It is like having a custom fitting suit versus a generic store bought suit. The custom suit fits you better because it is made just for you when the generic one is made for anyone who has similar body structure as you but not exactly like you.

Now to give you a more in-depth analysis, I will dive a little deeper into the product categories and talk about each of those and what and how they can vary by location. Typically, most convenience stores have products or departments for:

- ➢ Cigarettes and tobacco
- ➢ Beer and wine
- ➢ Drinks
- ➢ Grocery
- ➢ Automotive supplies and oil
- ➢ Deli food

Now I will take three gas stations in three vastly different neighborhoods and talk about how their product selections may vary from one to the other. Let's assume:

- ➢ Store one is an ethnic mixed inner city location
- ➢ Store two is located in a rural countryside location
- ➢ Store three is in the fancy part of your city

First, take store one for example. In the cigarette category you will carry more varieties of menthol type cigarettes, and then on the tobacco side, you will carry a selection of single cigars. In the beer and wine side, you will notice you are carrying more of a certain type of beer and wine that are mostly sold in a single can or bottle then your other store in the rural area.

Similarly, your grocery selection will vary widely too. In this store you may have to carry canned meat that is ready to eat, in the candy section, you will notice more of a selection of the candies that are less than a $1.00 each or sometimes bags of candy that are two for $1.00.

Now let's do the same for store two which is in a rural area. In this store your cigarettes will be mostly non-menthol, full flavored cigarettes that are subgeneric brands, as for tobacco, you will notice you sell mostly generic can tobacco and not much of single cigars. So you have to make room to put more of a selection of those in this store.

As for beer and wine, you will see you sell mostly bigger packages of cheaper beer like suitcases or eighteen-packs and not much of the smaller packages like six-packs. Similarly, all other product categories will be a little different than the previous one.

Now as for store three, your cigarette and tobacco will be different again. Here you may see you sell mostly high-value branded cigarettes like Marlboro and such and for tobacco, you will notice you sell the branded tobacco and good quality cigars.

On the beer side, you will notice you sell mostly high-end six-pack premium or imported beer versus generic cheaper beers. Same goes for wine; you will see that you sell a lot of $15 or higher valued wine bottles in this store. In grocery, you will sell mostly premium candy and gum and not much of the $1.00 value candies.

So as you can see there is no cookie cutter set up that fits every store; it is unique for each location and each business. One important thing to remember in this process is when you first merchandise your store based on your research; it is not done for good. You have to give it three months and then analyze your sales and go back and change things that need improvement.

Part of this improvement process is talking and getting feedback from your customers. It is a good idea to keep a log handy where every time a customer asks for something or look for items you don't carry, write them down so you can order them next time and let the customer know that you will carry the item just for them. This can make a customer feel important and valued, and trust me, he or she will be a loyal customer to your store for years to come.

We are not going to talk about the biggest product you carry in your store which is gasoline or fuel, yes it is part of what you sell, but since you cannot pick or choose what you can carry when it comes to fuel, we will not discuss it. But we will touch on this topic when we discuss pricing your products.

Let's recap what we've talked about so far. Regardless if you are merchandising a new store you just built, or if you are merchandising an existing store you just bought, remember, you are not alone in this. Some vendors will help you in this process, but you have to communicate with each and every one of those vendors and get their feedback and ask them what they sell the most in your neighborhood. This can give you a very good idea about how you need to set up your store.

So first you gather up information from those four items I mentioned regarding demographics. You get the median income of the people around you, find out their race and age and lastly determine if your store is a rural, city, or an inner city location.

Once you have all this information, you should have a rough idea based on our discussion as to what products you should concentrate on the most. Then you talk to your vendors and find out what they sell the most in their product line in your local neighborhood. If a vendor mentions he sells one hundred cases of something in a store twenty miles from you, don't pay attention, as that area may be entirely different than where you are. Ask them about your own neighborhood and not about the whole city.

As I said, you are not alone in this. Each of your vendors will guide you through this process, and remember, it is in their best interest also, if your sales are high in turn they are selling you more products, so it is a win-win situation for both. Their goal is to make you successful.

But before you start ordering your products, one last thing you need to do, visit your local competitors. Particularly the ones that seem successful or seem to be busy. Go see how they merchandise their store, make some mental notes and try to see if that jives with what you are going to do, if not you may have to rearrange yours a bit more.

Now, remember I said come back in three months and reevaluate your merchandising? Yes, in three months you need to sit down with all your invoices and look through and see what products in each category sold the most and what sold the least.

What you are trying to find out now is the sales per square foot. To figure this number out first, you need to know the square foot size of your sales floor and not the whole store. Let's say your sales floor is 1400 square feet, take your monthly sales without the fuel and divide that by the total sales for the month. So if you had $70,000 in sales the previous month, and you have 1400 square feet of sales floor, your sales per square foot are 70,000/1400 = 50. So your sales per square foot per month is $50. Now do that for every month.

Next, look through your shelves and merchandising, try to find items that are slow moving, meaning items that you order maybe once a month or less. Once you locate the slow moving items, remove them and try to bring in similar items that you think would be a good replacement for them. Similarly, if you notice you are ordering some items every week and still running out or running low, try to give them more visibility and room by giving them two shelf spaces instead of one. This way you are increasing the exposure of some of the high sellers.

Wait three months and go back and do this same process again and see if your sales per square foot increased or not. A typical rule of thumb is if your reorder frequency is six to eight weeks for most merchandise, then it is considered a slow seller. Your best bet would be to replace it with another item or just remove it all together. Remember, every time you pick out an item like that and replace it with a faster moving or selling item, your sales per square foot goes up, and in return, your profit goes up, so you make more money.

One important factor to keep in mind while deciding what and how to merchandise your store properly, there are grocery companies that you may want to hire who will supply you everything from cigarettes, tobacco, to motor oil. But when choosing the right company for you, it is best to meet with at least three to four of these companies and ask for their pricing book and then compare prices and product selections from each of them.

There are three types of grocery companies; one is national chains like McLane's, then there are regional companies like H.T. Hackney, and then there are some local companies based in or around where you are located. You can do a simple search or ask other vendors, and they will give you a few names and who to contact in these grocery companies.

Most or all of these companies provide you with experienced merchandisers who help you design and merchandise your store. But remember, even though they are experienced, they never do the research I outline in this book. So it is a good idea to do your research first, and then have an idea in mind before getting suggestions from any of these vendors.

Another reason you should have a grocery company to buy your merchandise from is that they keep up with the trends on what sells and what doesn't. Often times they will tell you about many upcoming new products that you can get in your store and be the first in your area to carry that product. So yes, there are benefits to having a company such as that. Another advantage is sometimes you will have products that didn't sell, or their shelf life expired, if you bought those from any grocery company, they will give you credit for those items and pick them up from your store.

Just remember, merchandising is an ongoing process. You have to make little changes every week and keep up with trends and new upcoming products.

BEST PRICING STRATEGY

Pricing is one of the most important factors of your business. A carefully thought out pricing strategy can make you very successful, but a pricing strategy that places you above your market can literality put you out of business. Pricing below the market can wipe your bottom line profit completely clean, and before you know it, you are out of business and in debt. That is the risky part.

Now the tricky part is, if you stay with the market, then you are NOT standing out in the crowd. Instead, you are standing in the crowd. To make yourself more visible and unique and to stand tall among other competitors, you have to be very creative when it comes to your pricing strategy, and that is where the tricky part comes in. My goal is to teach you how to implement a carefully thought out pricing strategy that can make you stand out and make you successful.

First, we want to discuss your buying price or the price you pay when you buy your inventory. Because if you don't buy at the lowest possible price then you won't be able to sell them at a competitive price, nor will you be able to keep your margin. So it is vital that you negotiate hard and get the lowest possible price.

If you recall, I spoke about grocery companies. They supply you with 60% of your in-store merchandise; this is where your negotiation should start. Picking the right company to buy from can make a huge difference in your bottom line. Even a ten cent difference in a carton of cigarettes makes a significant impact on your bottom line profit. Here is how.

Say you buy 200 cartons of cigarettes a week, and at fifteen cents higher cost you will be paying $30 a week which translates into $130 a month and $1,560 a year! When calculating weekly, monthly and yearly, it is a good idea to calculate everything based on 52 weeks for the year and 4.34 weeks in a month. So as you can see, just a dime and a nickel in price difference can make a huge impact in this case.

If you have Sam's Club or Costco type wholesaler in your area, go to them and see their wholesale cigarette prices first as they are known to be cheaper compared to most other grocery companies. Then sit down with at least three to four grocery companies and compare their prices and see who offers you the best prices. Let them tell you their lowest price in writing first, then offer them a dime less than what they offered and tell them if they can make that happen they will have a deal.

Keep in mind, cigarettes are the most competitive commodity when it comes to pricing so don't expect much; they may come down another three to four cents if that. Now if you see they are still the lowest compared to the local Sam's Club and other grocery companies, then you should go with them. Provided they are offering you competitive prices on other grocery items as well.

If you remember where I spoke about how to pick the right grocery company? Best is to get each of those company's price book and put them side by side and then compare apple to apple and orange to orange. Meaning you should pick out a few items from the candy section and match those prices, and then similarly do the same for cookies, cakes, automotive accessories, oil, and drinks and so on.

Keep in mind you will not find any company who has lower prices on every item, as long as they are lower on most items, then you should be good. One more thing to look for, sometimes these companies offer lower cigarettes prices to get your business while they charge higher prices on every other item from tobacco to drinks, so it is important to check all other categories and make sure they are competitive in other areas too.

Since we are talking about cigarettes and tobacco, next, you need to meet with the tobacco manufacturer sales reps, and it is imperative that you build a stable relationship with them as they are the ones who offer you some type of contract where they compensate you for promoting their cigarette and tobacco products.

Since the recent merger between Lorillard and RJ Reynolds in 2015, you most likely have to deal with just two companies and not three anymore. Depending on your store's location, one of these companies will have a more dominant presence compared to the other. Do your market research and know where you should be when it comes to pricing your cigarettes and tobacco.

Know your competitor's prices so you can stay in line with them. Also, talk to your sales reps from Phillip Morris and RJ Reynolds and see what the biggest contract you can get from each of them. As in this case, larger or higher level contracts, when it comes to cigarette companies, translate into bigger and deeper discounts. Meaning they pay you more money per pack cash discount. So negotiate for higher discount and not lower.

Next, you have to sit down with your local Coca-Cola and Pepsi sales people. See what programs they have to offer you. Lately, both of these companies have started to push out contracts where they take a certain percentage of your cooler space and in exchange they offer you cheaper contract pricing. But the downside is often times they try to enforce the selling price too. An example is Coke recently offered a case of twelve-ounce cans which has four six-packs for around $8, or $2 for each six-pack. But in order for you to buy them at that price, you would have to agree to sell them for $2.25 for each six-pack or $9 a case. In my twenty plus years experience, I have always seen around 33%-35% profit margin in the soda/drinks category/department. But when you run specials such as this, that 35% margin goes down to 28%-30%, which can be a significant dollar amount.

For example, say your store sells around $400 of soda and drinks a day, which is $12,000 a month, and if your profit margin is 35% then your monthly profit dollar is $4,200 a month. Now let's take a look at the profit margin when it is down to say 30% because you ran too many low margin promotions. The same sale would bring you $3,600, which is a difference of $600 each month and in a years' time, which equals $7,200.

But don't think I am against all promotions. I love promotions, as that is how you grow your business. But there is a fine line between running a limited time offering and running a year around low-priced promotion where people expect you to sell that product at those low prices. A true promotion should always be for a limited time and not always on the same or similar items. Your goal is not to have your customers expecting $2.25 for a six-pack all year around. When something great is given to us more often than usual, we become used to it, and our brain is trained to expect it instead of appreciating it. You want your customers to enjoy a promotion but not expect it each time they visit your store.

Remember, your store is a convenience store and not a discount grocery store. When a customer walks into a gas station or convenience store, they know they may pay a little higher for a pack of cigarettes or a candy bar compared to if they walked into their local grocery store or the discount warehouse.

They pay for that convenience of walking only five steps from their car to buy the item; they pay for that fast in and out convenience. Not to mention they pay for that convenience of shopping at your store at two in the morning when most other big retail chains are closed.

Now let's recap, meet with the sales people of both Coke and Pepsi and negotiate for the best suitable contract for you. Remember not to sign the first day you meet, take note when you meet with them, review the information, and then get back to them to negotiate.

Now a few companies you can't negotiate with. For example, Frito-Lay and most other chip companies won't negotiate prices as they have set prices. No worry, you pay the same price what Wal-Mart pays for those chips. The only difference is some of these companies do offer you a percentage of the total sales back to you as a rebate if you are part of any large chain stores, or you belong to a buying group. The next non-negotiable category is beer and wine. In most states, if not all, beer is distributed by only a handful of companies.

For example, Budweiser or Miller beer is produced and sold by one company in one area or city, and since no other company is producing or selling the same beer, there is no price competition nor are there any price negotiations. I will cover this topic later on.

Next, you need to meet and negotiate with some of the smaller vendors such as the ice company if your store sells ice. Then the company that sells you coffee, cakes, and other snack items. Most of these smaller companies will negotiate with you so make sure to talk to some of your competitors as well and pick the best and least expensive one as long as the products they are selling are the same or equal quality.

Now that you are buying your merchandise at the lowest possible price let's talk about the other half of the equation, the selling price.

First, let me address cigarettes and tobacco again, if you are in a contract with both of the tobacco companies, then you have some guidelines that you have to maintain. More importantly, your cigarette and tobacco prices are determined by how much your competitors are selling them for.

People are more price conscious when it comes to their cigarettes especially since they buy the same thing or same cigarettes every day. They know and remember that price well, so try not to price yourself out of the market here, try to stay within the market range. A difference of five to ten cents is okay but not fifty cents. Just remember this is the category you have to be very competitive at.

Next, soda and drinks. Again, 99% of gas stations in any area sell their twenty-ounce Coke or Pepsi at a set price, so you can't play the pricing game here. The only price game here is for milk or other soft drinks that are not Coke or Pepsi. You can also run various other promotions on the bigger packages like a twelve-pack of cans or two-liter bottle sodas.

Chips and similar products usually have a price printed on them, so no room to play there either. Move on to some other smaller items like a bag of ice, snack cakes, coffee, and fountain drinks. This is where you need to be creative and make yourself visible among other retailers. Run great promotions year around but on different items. In winter, run a special on coffee or cappuccino, and in the summer months run a special on fountain drinks.

The store, 7-Eleven, does a wonderful job when it comes to summer fountain drink promotions. They always promote a sixty-four-ounce huge mug for a very low price, and the deal is every time you bring that big mug back to the store for a refill, you only pay a few cents. They created a huge fan base that carries those mugs and visits 7-Eleven every day even if they have to go out of their way to get to one of those stores. That is what brand loyalty is. You don't have to copy their exact model, but you can produce some creative promotions that go better for your local neighborhood's needs.

In the beer and wine category, as I said, you most likely won't be able to negotiate any prices, but you can always entertain some deals. For example, Budweiser and Miller both often offer case deals, where if you buy fifty or one hundred cases of the same package, they may offer $1-$2.50 off each case. These two companies always have some type of promotions going on, but not all of them are great promotions for every store.

When it comes to selling prices, this is where you have to be very creative. Again, check your local area competitors and then decide where you need to be. But remember, if you are already offering the cheapest fuel or cigarette prices, there is no reason for you to offer the cheapest beer also. Instead, use one of the items in your store as the loss leader to bring people in and keep the rest of your merchandise at regular prices.

If you have a grocery company to supply you with all your grocery, tobacco, cigarettes, drinks, and candy items, then pricing can be easier for you. Usually, when you sign up with your grocery company, they always ask you what type of profit margin you want to keep in each category. It can reduce your work as the grocery company will process each grocery item before shipping them to you, and all those grocery items will be pre-priced at your desired profit margin. Similarly, they will suggest prices on the invoice for your candy, drinks, and all other items. It is then up to you to decide if you want to follow their suggested retail prices or not.

Remember, you can always adjust the suggested retail price by contacting your grocery company. This is the profit margin I tell my grocery company to price my merchandise at:

- Grocery at 35%
- Candy at 40%
- Automotive Accessories & oil at 50%
- Drinks at 37%
- Tobacco at 25%
- Deli food at 50%
- Cigarettes at 17%

FUEL PRICING

Now let's talk about buying and selling fuel, which is your biggest category really. When it comes to buying your fuel, I am sure 95% of you out there are already locked into a fuel supply agreement or contract. If you are, then you can't pick and choose your suppliers like you can for your grocery items.

But don't feel bad, most all fuel suppliers have standard contracts, where they sell you fuel at a penny or two over the rack price. Let me explain what rack price is first. Rack price is the published wholesale fuel price for a specific day and area, and it can vary by brands, location, and it varies day to day. Fuel is a commodity, and like any other commodity fuel gets traded daily, and prices do go up and down by supply and demand. Let's say the rack price today for Chevron in your area is $2.00 per gallon.

If you buy gasoline today, your supplier will charge you $2.00 for each gallon, along with all the local, federal, and state taxes. Lastly, based on your contract with them, they will add anywhere from zero to four cents to each gallon as their profit. Now, how much they add will depend on what you negotiated with them when you signed that fuel contract. It is always a good idea to know your contract well. This way you know how much more you may be paying compared to your competitors. I will get into more details about fuel contracts when we cover vendor contracts later on.

Now if you don't have a fuel contract or if you are building a new station or buying a station that comes without a fuel contract, you are in the driver's seat, and you should negotiate a good solid contract that benefits you in the long run. Remember, a typical fuel contract usually runs for ten years or more. So negotiate hard as you have to abide by that contract for a long time to come. As I said, I will cover contract negotiation later on.

Now let's talk about pricing your fuel. Remember, pricing your fuel is most likely THE most important pricing strategy you will ever make for your business, so be careful and do not take this lightly.

Pricing your fuel is not like pricing your grocery, cigarettes, or soda. There is no set margin or set pricing for fuel. Just as the buying price varies with the market, selling prices do too. It is best to do a price survey daily of at least three to four of your nearest competitors, this way you can see where you should price yours.

But before you price your fuel, first you need to figure out who the leader in your area is. Rank each station including yourself, this way you know who to follow and who will follow you. If you have a national brand or a very dominating station near you, then put them at rank one, then see who should be number two and so on. If you decide you are the dominating brand in your neighborhood, then you are in a very good place as you can dictate the market. But if it is someone else then be careful and price accordingly.

Some of the dominating brands have a tendency to be the lowest. If you have one of those, then make sure to stay a penny or two above them. The last thing you want is to start a price war between you and them where at the end you will be the one losing everything since they tend to have deeper pockets.

2. PEOPLE AKA HIRED HELP

Let me first answer a very common question that most small business owners ask. Which is how to find, hire, train, and retain the right people? I will try to answer that question along with a step by step process for you to follow for all your staffing needs.

It is a huge topic and a critical one. You can have the best location and lowest priced products, but without the right people behind your register, you won't be able to sell anything. The proper staffing is one of the vital keys to your success. I broke this staffing part into a ten-step process, and I will discuss each in detail.

WHERE AND HOW TO FIND THE RIGHT PEOPLE TO HIRE

Often I am sure every one of us has walked into a store and saw a notice on the front door that says "Now Hiring" for a small retail business such as a gas station. In my opinion, it is not a good idea. Why? Well, your target audience, in this case, is your surrounding neighborhood, so most of the applications that you will get are from the neighborhood.

Let's say you get ten applications, and you meet and interview each of them, and end up hiring one person out of the ten. Chances are you may alienate the other nine and some of those people who were your customers, at first, may not come to visit you afterward, simply because you didn't hire them.

Best practices to hire people are through advertising in a way that covers your city or locality and not just in your neighborhood. I have three suggestions on where to advertise and find people.

A. Run an ad on Craigslist. You may be surprised how often people look for jobs on Craigslist. Craigslist is an essential tool for a lot of things, from selling your old couch or bicycle to hiring people to do your yard or carpentry work to hiring new employees. I use Craigslist every time I need help; I even hired an excellent bookkeeper from there.

B. Word of mouth. You can ask some of your other employees if they know of any competent and decent people they can recommend. Ask your friends or other business owners that you know well, this way you, at least, have a reference where they are coming from.

C. Hiring employees from other local retailers. Sounds bad I know, but again remember, you are not doing anything illegal or unethical. Let me explain. You go to your local burger joint, and the lady that took your order was very courteous and professional. Strike up a conversation with her, compliment her on her professionalism let her know you own such and such business, and you are looking to hire some decent employees.

Ask her if she knows anyone that she can recommend. Give her your business card. You will see out of five people you meet this way, three will call you either with a recommendation, or they will call to apply for themselves. There are three reasons she may contact you. First, obviously people love compliments, second, most employees do not feel appreciated enough at their current jobs, and third, everyone wants to move up at their job and eventually make more money. So take advantage of that.

Now that you have some applicants calling you, you need to give them each an application, right? Where do you get these job applications? I am sure you can go to the local office supply store and pick a stack of them up but is that a good idea? The answer is no. Those applications are very generic and not designed for your type of business.

So it's best to create one or modify an existing one you may already have that fits your needs. You can also go to my blog, (http://GasStationBusiness101.com) and you will find a generic job application under the Resource tab that you can download and modify for your own needs. When preparing a job application, a few things to keep in mind. Absolutely no social security number on the application. It is also a good idea not to ask about race on a job application.

Make sure to ask about their education level, previous employment history, along with how many addresses they've had in the last five years. These three things can tell you a lot about a person. If an applicant held one job for the last five years, lived in one address in that five years and had a high school education, chances are, he or she will be a good employee. Compared to an applicant that had four jobs in the last five years, moved three times in that same period, and does not have a high school diploma.

When asking about previous employment, make sure to ask the name and contact information of the company along with the name of their supervisors. This way you can check their references. Remember, it is a common practice for employers not to reveal any details of a current or former employee. So if you ask were they good or bad at their job, you may not get an answer, you may just have to read (hear in this case) between the lines. But they all can say if that person can be rehired or not. Your answer lies in that answer if they say he or she can be rehired, you know they are saying they do recommend that person.

ASKING THE RIGHT QUESTIONS DURING AN INTERVIEW

Once you find some decent applicants, call a few of them for an interview. I always give them a simple math test to see if they can calculate basic addition and subtraction in their head. It is a good idea to ask a few hypothetical questions ranging from how to handle a customer service issue to an emergency situation. If someone were to get sick inside, how would they handle that emergency?

Watch and listen and see if they use a common sense approach to answering them or not. Then I ask them if they have any physical limitations which may prevent them from performing the normal duties and responsibilities of the store's work, and if they are able to pick up thirty pounds or not. Remember, it is important, as any typical gas stations garbage can, when full, weigh as much as twenty-five to thirty pounds, so it is important to know if they can or not.

But remember, you cannot discriminate if they cannot lift that weight, but as long as you know they can't, you can arrange someone else to pick that up.

Next, I usually ask if they can bring a background check of themselves from the local police dept, and I do offer to pay for that cost. It saves money and time to have them provide you with that report instead of you running a background check on them. Once all these things check out, go ahead and hire them. One more thing to make clear right before you hire them, do let them know that it is your company policy to hire people with a 60 to a 90-day probation period. Meaning, they can be let go anytime during those 60 to 90 days without giving them any reasons based on their performance.

Once you hire them, there is some basic paperwork that you need to give them to fill out. I am sure everyone of you that is in business has a set of paperwork that you give your new hire. But I would still like to go through a checklist of some paperwork I give to my new hires so you can match them with yours.

➢ The completed job application that you already have

➢ W-2 from the IRS

➢ New hire handbook (If you are a branded station, your oil company usually provides you with some basic training material to hand out to each new hire)

- A disclaimer about the 60 to 90-day probation period (Where I explain for the next 60 to 90 days they are on probation, their job can be terminated based on poor performance, and I have them sign it)

- Their criminal background check that they brought, keep it in their personnel file

- Copy of their social security card and driver's license or state identification card

- Store key responsibility acknowledgment (In this one-page acknowledgment consent, I want each employee to sign stating that they understand the true responsibility of safeguarding the store key)

Remember some states require you to register all new employees you hire with the Department of Labor within seven days of hiring if not there will be a fine imposed on you. So check with your state's DOL and see if they require it. One more thing you need to find out about your state is if your state is an employment at will state or not.

Alabama, among many other states, is an employment at will state. Meaning you can terminate anyone anytime without giving them any reason. Yes, it sounds odd I know, and maybe I am oversimplifying it, but the essence is that you really do not have to give them much of a reason for the termination.

Once you hire an employee, it is important to provide them with proper training. First, give them a walk around the store and show them what you sell and how to stock them, how you merchandise them. Then show them how to restock the shelves and the coolers and how often that should be done. It is a good idea to have a checklist that you can hand them which details a typical cashier's job duties and responsibilities, what is expected of them before they start their shift and after they close their shift. I usually provide three full days of training before I let any new employee work or run a shift all by themselves.

The first day, I show them around then I put them with an experienced cashier so they can observe the operation of the cash register for at least two hours without touching the register at all. The second half of the day I let them get more hands-on training where they will start doing the transaction while the trainer stands next to them and guides them through each step.

The second day, I again explain the checklist and let them do the pre-shift chores, which usually involves restocking the coolers before taking over the shifts. Making sure the fountain and coffee area is fully stocked, then they can go do a shift again with a trainer, but today they have to take the lead while the trainer will stand next to them.

The third day, they will be totally on their own even though there is a trainer, but not next to them. Instead, I tell the trainer to go do other things away from the checkout stand so they can observe the new hire from a distance and see how they are doing. The new hire is only allowed to call the trainer when he or she is completely stuck.

After the third day is complete, then judging by how well the new hire did, we decide if they need one extra day of training, or if they are ready to go on their own. Though, not often but it has happened a few times, where after the second or third day of training either the new hire decided not to work anymore, or we decided that this person won't be able to handle this task or the job.

Once we know that fact, we do not continue the training. Instead we just tell them it will not work while explaining to them the reasons we didn't think they are a good fit for our store.

EMPLOYEE APPEARANCE

Appearance is the most important first impression on your customer. You do not get a second chance to create that first impression, so make sure your employees are in a uniform of some sort. If you are a branded store like Shell, BP, Chevron, or such, then you have a uniform that you provide your employees along with a name tag.

But what if you are a non-branded store? Like a Mike's Mini-Mart or such, you can still get some uniform for them. Go to your local screen printing store, and you can get t-shirts with your logo and name printed on them for a very nominal price. One quick note on that, if you don't have a logo for your store, you can go online to Fiverr.com and pay $5 and get a logo created for you. There is no reason not to be professional and making sure your store and employees look just as professional as branded store employees.

MOTIVATING AND EMPOWERING YOUR EMPLOYEES

You need to make sure your employees do not feel that this is a dead end job. To do so, you need to motivate them. Typically, there are three ways that you can motivate your employees.

1. By showing them the ladder, they can climb to be a manager one day. From the cashier, to shift leader, to shift manager to assistant manager, and then finally store manager one day. Let them know that it is possible with hard work and dedication.

2. Tell them the way you increase their pay. I typically tell all new hires that I would start them at a certain hourly rate then after 60 days they will get a raise to a certain hourly rate and every six months I will do a performance review of them, and if I see they are performing well, they will get a raise. You can tell them it will be every nine months or every three months. It is totally up to you.

3. Another great way to motivate your staff is just simply by telling them they are doing a great job. Give them a compliment when you see good work, acknowledge it and show them you noticed. A simple "thank you," or a pat on the back can go a long way sometimes. Remember, everybody wants to feel appreciated.

TEACHING THEM MARKETING 101

In this step, your team needs to know your marketing strategy so they can promote your store and certain products. Let me explain, say you have a special on 2-liter soda for ninety-nine cents this month, if you want to promote it, it needs little more than a sign on the back of the store. Think if your employee mentioned this to each of the clients this week or this month.

You have 2-liters of soda for ninety-nine cents. Two out of five customers may buy that; it is that simple. Another example, say you have a two-pack cigarette special where you give a lighter for free. Ask your employees to mention that to anyone buying a single pack of cigarettes.

See how many of them end up buying two packs instead, you will be surprised. More than 50% will go for the two-pack special. The power of face to face marketing can be a very powerful thing.

REWARDING THE RIGHT BEHAVIOR

If you see an employee doing a great job handling a bad situation at work, or they showed some exceptional quality or ability which is beyond their daily work duties and responsibilities, reward them by at least acknowledging their work or effort. Buy them lunch or sit down and have lunch with him or her, it can mean a lot to them. Give them a gift certificate for a movie or pizza, anything small like that can make them feel appreciated and proud of being a part of your team.

HOW TO DISCIPLINE BAD BEHAVIOR

Now let's face the truth, we don't always get the best employees, there are bad apples in every bunch right? Now how do you discipline bad behavior when you see it? It could be not doing their job properly, giving poor customer service, not doing their side work, or even showing up to work late more than once in the same week. Nothing too serious.

Let me just say here, if you see truly bad behavior or a violation of your company policy or even subordination when you asked them to perform a duty, and they refuse, these are grounds for immediate termination and not a disciplinary action. But for minor issues like I mentioned earlier, you can give them a verbal warning first and monitor them to see if there is any improvement if not, you can then give them a written warning.

Most stores have these forms of written warnings where you fill in the action that they took which was not proper or the job that they did not perform even after a prior verbal warning. Once you give them a copy of that, ask them to sign it and keep a copy of it in their personnel file. I usually terminate an employee if he or she makes the same violation within 30 days of giving them the written warning.

SETTING UP TARGET & GOAL ORIENTED INCENTIVES

I do this often in my stores. I set up individual goals and offer incentives if they reach the goal. I am sure you are wondering what and how. I had a store with a car wash, where the carwash prices were set at $2 for basic, $4 for the medium grade wash and $7 for the works, the ultimate wash. I set up a plan where every time a cashier sold any of the medium level wash they would get $.50 cents, and if they sold any $7 wash, I would pay them $1 for each wash sold.

As long as they keep each receipt and sign their name on the ticket. Every week I would pay them. Before this incentive program, my monthly carwash sales were around $2,000 a month. Once I started it, from the very next month, my carwash sales rose to around $3,500 to as high as $5,400 one month.

You can be very creative when it comes to creating an incentive program, but it depends on what you sell in your store. I have done the same with Deli food, where I set up a daily target and a weekly target, and if they reached that goal, each employee got an incentive pay.

REGULAR EMPLOYEE MEETINGS AND COACHING

Last but not least, it is very important to have regularly scheduled employee meetings and coaching. Meet every month, where you tell them of any upcoming changes in your store, and then ask for any issues they faced that month or any concerns they have.

This is also the time to roll out any new incentive plans you have for them for the following month. Offer them tips, words of encouragement, and remind them to greet and make eye contact with each customer. Also, emphasize the restroom cleaning regime and keeping the coffee and fountain areas clean.

3. MARKETING & PROMOTION

In this 21st century, marketing and promotion for brick and mortar businesses have changed a whole lot. It's not all about just in-store or local area marketing; it is about online marketing too. Local businesses are benefiting from online marketing, and that is why most big chain retailers spend two to three times as much money on online marketing than offline or local area marketing, so my advice is so, should you.

Any retail store operator understands the importance of marketing. Unless you are reaching out to your target audience, how can you expect them to become customers? Having a few lucky patrons is not going to keep you in business and certainly not lead to a lot of profits. If the local community is engaged effectively and positively, it can help create opportunities for the company to grow.

However, for that to happen, it is important to understand about local area marketing and using the right tactics and techniques. Local area marketing can help you to create local buzz and interest for your store. If you reach out to your local community and show them what you are offering, it is very likely that they will come to you for their purchasing. However, keep in mind all of this requires constant effort to attract people to you. Understanding your local community and target market is also paramount.

The opportunities that it presents are unlimited. When you start marketing to your local community, you can start developing relationships on a personal level, which means you can increase your chances of business as you are able to become a favorable retailer in the eyes of your community. They can also help spread the word about your business thus increasing and contributing to expanding your influence. To effectively market yourself locally, here are some things that you can do.

ORGANIZE AN EVENT

Whether it is an awareness session or an annual sale, events are a great way for the community to gather everyone to generate interest in your business. It also provides a great opportunity for the business executives to meet their customers and allow them to know you better. Today, business is more about relationships, and if you are not able to maintain healthy relationships with your customers, then you can wave them off to your competitor.

Doing business has become tough in today's competitive environment. Any business that thinks they still have the power to influence their customer's decision is wrong. Very little power lies with retailers; most of the power rests with consumers.

With today's technological advancements, bulk productions, competitive prices, advertising, and the number of choices available, consumers have become aware. They are not influenced by the marketer or retailer today, but instead, they are able to make their own decisions.

Consumers have begun to understand the marketing tactics of retailers and have become smart. In this situation, have you become smarter than your customer? Most likely not. So creating meaningful contact and relationships has become more important to do business and the starting point is trust.

If you want to grow and make more sales, you have to inculcate a trustful relationship with your customers. When they trust you only then, they will feel comfortable in conducting business with you. This also means that you should be creating a valuable exchange with them; provide them some kind of value, something of interest to them. In return, your customer will then respond by reacting to your sale offer. However, keep in mind that this is a slow and steady process. You have to keep nurturing your relationship to build it to the level that it reaps favorable results.

Another idea is to sponsor any local event in your area, such as a local school kids' baseball, football, or softball games. You can also cater some food and drinks for a Sunday service at your local church. Typically, these types of sponsorships do not cost much but get your name out there as a productive member of your local community.

CREATE PARTNERSHIPS

A business can also build partnerships with other local businesses or non-business organizations to become active and get noticed in the local community. It will help give a boost to your company, and you can also participate in local community events this way.

For example, a business can collaborate with the local school program or function where they can play an active and productive role. However, keep in mind your target audience while doing this. For example, if your target audience isn't directly children but their parents, still forming a partnership with the school for any event will help get you noticed by the parents if they are also attending. Tactics such as this help raise local awareness of the business.

PERSONAL INTRODUCTIONS

If you want to grow your local influence, another good strategy, which is also becoming increasingly popular among entrepreneurs, is personal introductions. Make it a point to introduce your business to at least five people each week in person. Whether it is in your store, at the local bar or another place where you know your target audience is likely to hang out. Giving them your business card is an effective marketing strategy.

When you can form a relationship with someone at a personal level, chances are they are more likely to shop at your store or at least try it out. If they like it, they are more likely to refer other people to it. So suppose you meet 250 new people in a year, chances are at least 50 of them will become your customer or spread the word about your business to others.

By personally putting yourself out there, you are giving them an opportunity to talk about you. Even if they don't become your customer, they are likely to tell others about their encounter with you and in doing so; they will end up talking about your business or store.

OFFER EXCLUSIVE DISCOUNTS

If your store is located somewhere near a major employer, you can offer discounts or offers to their employees. This is also a good way to generate local buzz because that way you are not only targeting local employees but also their families. You may be offering a discount only to them, but they are more likely to bring their family over as well if they have a positive experience with your brand. Making the local employees, your VIP customer is also a good strategy. By distributing VIP cards through the employer for their employees, you can enhance your chances of being paid a visit by those who haven't tried your store out before.

Whether or not you are holding regular company events, you should, at least, take part in the local fundraisers and activities whether or not you are formally invited. As a company, you should be doing everything in your power to attract local attention and generate buzz. Your creativity is only limited by your imagination.

If you know a local event or carnival is taking place, you can hand out your company brochures or offer discounts as a way to attract people. Even a minimal discount could mean that you will, at least, attract some part of that audience which you were targeting. Marketing strategies don't take a lot of time, but they require constant action and attention. You can expect to be active in one event and forget about the other. However, it also does not mean that you forget about the costs associated with engaging in these events. Find the most relevant events that your company should participate in, and from there start engaging in reverse order. This approach can help you balance your costs with the benefits.

However, also, keep in mind that not all marketing need to be expensive. We are not talking about big budgets and booking billboards. You can do that if you have the budget, but focus on creating relationships on a personal level with your community to enhance your local influence. Companies that have a substantial stronghold locally are better able to market themselves globally. By using strategies to attract local consumers, you can also better understand your local demographics and strategize on a bigger scale accordingly.

Data and consumer insights are critical in marketing, and when you are successful in attracting your local consumers, you are more confident to take your marketing to the global level. There are many opportunities for a company to grown and increase its profit margins, but it comes with constant effort and patience on the part of the company.

Creating customer engagement is the first step in developing trust and relationships with your target audience. While you're marketing locally, take the opportunity to know your customers better. Understanding how your customers make decisions and how their psyche works when it comes to purchasing from your store will give you insights into what products you should stock, how you should stock them, and what more you can offer to them to create a positive experience. All these things together play their role in helping a retail business grow and enhance its bottom line profit margin.

Before you start a big promotion at your business, it is a good idea to take a look at the sales ratio of different categories in your store. This way you can find out which categories are strong and which ones aren't this way can you target those weaker ones and promote them. Here is an example of a typical mom and pop gas station and convenience store.

Typically, at a gas station or neighborhood store, this is how the category breakdown looks regarding sales ratio.

➢ Cigarettes: 30-35%
➢ Tobacco: 6-7%
➢ Soda/Drinks: 17-19%
➢ Beer/Wine: 15-20%
➢ Deli: 10-15%
➢ Grocery: 10-15%

Remember, some of these percentages can vary widely depending on where you are located. For example, a rural area store may sell more cigarettes and beer than a heart of the city location. On the other hand, a gas station in New York City or San Diego may sell 10%-15% cigarettes compared to 35%-40% in a small town in North Carolina. So it all depends on where you are. Based on your location and trends, write down your percentage of sales and figure out your strongest to weakest categories.

Another good example is a beef brisket sandwich that we used to sell at Quiznos. Though it was our number one seller in the south, nationwide, it was not a top seller. So the corporate marketing team took it off the menu, and our sales tanked. The point I am trying to make is that depending on what and where you are selling, some items in your store can be great sellers, and some will not be as strong even though they may have a healthy sales number in other parts of the country. So know your market well and out your winners and losers. This way your job as a business owner becomes easier.

3 IN-STORE PROMOTION IDEAS

When you first start your store promotions, try not to do too many promotions at once, if you do it will be hard for you to track which promotion worked better for you. It is also called the split testing or A-B testing. In this process, you test product 'A' for three weeks and see how people are responding to that sale. Then stop that sale and start the sale on Product 'B' for three weeks, at the end see which of these two products gave you a better result.

PRODUCTS PROMOTION

In this type of promotion, you promote your products such as buy one get one free or BOGO or similar type of advertising. Often, these types of promotions work wonders for most businesses.

PRICE PROMOTION

This promotion is the easiest to do but the hardest to manage. It is easy to slash prices on products, merchandise, or fuel, but hard to manage because by reducing the price you are also reducing your bottom line profit dollars. So if you are not careful, you can end up in the red before you know it.

PROMOTION VIA PEOPLE OR EMPLOYEES

This is where you promote your business through your employees, by word of mouth, hopefully, good word of mouth. Suggestive selling, where your employees suggest a product or food items by saying, "Have you tried our sandwiches or the new coffee cakes we just got it? They are very popular." Trust me, a statement such as that can work wonders.

You and your employees can also do some local area marketing, where you go meet other local businesses, churches, or local kids' baseball teams and introduce yourself and tell them what your business offers and how they can benefit from trading with you. Offer them some type of incentives; tell them they can have free coffee or a fountain drink if they come visit you at the store.

Out of the three types of promotions, in my opinion, this is by far the best way to promote your business, especially if you can use this method in conjunction with one of the other ones. Let me explain; say you are doing a BOGO special on 2-liter bottles of Coke. If your employees mention that to every customer that comes through your door every day, you will sell three times more than if they didn't mention that to the customers.

Remember I said I always split test my promotions? I did this exact test in one of my stores a couple of years ago, where I had a BOGO 2-liter special. We started the promotion on a Monday, and then I told my employees to mention the sale to each and every customer that came through the door the next day which was Tuesday, come Wednesday, I told everyone not to say a word about the promotion to any customers. Even though Coke did put up a big sign in two different places inside the store which was hard to miss.

This was the result I recorded. The Monday we started the sale, we sold 32 bottles all day when no one mentioned anything to the customers. The second day we sold 134 bottles, this was the day every employee said it to every customer that came through the door. The third day (Wednesday) no one mentioned the sale, and we ended up selling 76 bottles, and I need to mention here that we had 20 customers that came in on Wednesday and asked if we still had the promotion. Out of that 20, 16 were new customers meaning they did not visit us Tuesday. So they came via word of mouth. See how convincing your employees can be when you combine this with a product or price promotion? Go try one, and you will see it for yourself.

Once you know your weakest category, then it's time for you to decide how aggressive you want to be. But remember, nothing will give you an overnight result. A good marketing promotion strategy takes time to produce results. If you are not hard pressed for sales, then take it easy and identify the weakest category out of those six main ones, and then decide what would be a good promotional strategy for that category.

Here is a great example of an effective promotion and marketing campaign that 7-Eleven does every year. They promote fountain drinks during summer and coffee or cappuccino in the winter. You can always start a promotion like that and advertise it well and let your employees mention it to every customer.

Remember not to run too many specials at once, you don't want your employees to mention a laundry list of promotions to each customer, nor do you want them to mention some type of promotion every time a customer walks in. If you do that, then most of your regular customers will learn to tune that sales pitch out. Just put yourself in a customer's place, no one wants to hear a sales pitch every time they walk into a store every day. So make it a once a week thing and not an everyday thing.

Now, if you work through your categories and start promoting the weakest one, what will eventually happen is you are going to make your most vulnerable category turn into a strong one.

Essentially, this is how you grow your business. Remember the BOGO special can increase your sales for a few days or until the promotion lasts.

Once the sale ends, your sales will go back down to what it was before. But if you do smaller promotions in a particular category, more people/customers will discover that you carry such and such products at a reasonable price and will become your regular customers. Targeting your weakest category cannot only make you gain more business but more sales dollars that you never had, to begin with.

Let's say you have lower back pain and a weak knee, and you go to a fitness professional to get fit, and after doing various tests he or she tells you, you first have to strengthen your back and knee muscles before you can do a regular workout or weight training. Just like your body, your business needs work on the weakest links or areas first.

Now for those of you who are in the gas station business, you can also promote fuel. That big gas price sign you have is one of the most powerful marketing tools you have at your disposal. But you have to use it very carefully as it can make you rich or break your bank if done wrong. If you want a quick boost in your business, lower your fuel price by two cents below your competitors and see how people react. But as I said, it is a very slippery slope which you don't want to go down. Instead, find out who the fuel market leader (the station that sells the most fuel) is in your area, and then figure out how aggressive they are and price your station accordingly.

But as I said, sometimes to create a buzz or a quick boost you can go two to three cents below your competitors but only for a weekend or so. Just remember, there is always that risk that the leader will come down and match you or even go down below your selling price and if they do, you are doomed. So play it very carefully, or you can take the whole market down with you.

When I want to promote a new store or a store that is under-performing, I usually contact local middle schools and see if kids are interested in doing a carwash to raise money for their school or church, where I provide them with water and sometimes even soap and some supplies. I do it on a Friday afternoon and all day Saturday.

This is when I would drop my fuel price (just regular-unleaded) two to three cents below everyone around me. Then, I also bring in a hot dog cart where we grill hot dogs, sausage dogs, and offer $1.99 deal for a hot dog and a fountain drink. The trick here is I sell the hot dog from the cart outside but for the drink; they would have to walk inside the store. My goal is to get them inside so they may end up buying more items.

What this type of promotion does is creates a buzz among your locality, and you end up gaining a few new customers. Even though to do such a promotion it usually costs me around $400-$500 for those two days. But to me, that money is well spent. I calculate it like this; say I gained 40 new customers from this two-day event. Then my customer acquisition cost is 450/40 = $11.25 right?

That seems high at first I am sure, but let's take a look at an average merchandise sale ticket in an average convenience store, which is around $5-$7. So say it is $6, and these 40 new customers visit my store three times a week which is the average for most customers. So each customer is spending $18 a week and $78.12 each month, right? So at 27% profit margin, I am making $21.09 from each customer. I didn't even calculate the fuel profit yet but see how in a little over two weeks I recouped that $11.25 customer acquisition cost, and after that every time they visit out store it is all profit. Remember, sometimes you have to spend money to make money.

Another trick you can use while doing product promotion is offer bundle prices. Anyone buying a pack of cigarettes, offer them a two or three pack special instead where you take off a nickel from each pack. Remember, people in general like the idea of saving money. So when your employees offer that, four out of five will go for it.

I do a little more creative promotion when it comes to cigarettes. Instead of offering a nickel discount on each pack, I offer a three pack deal with a lighter free, and it does work wonders. When you are offering fifteen cents off on a three pack that does not sound like much of a discount does it? But a free lighter? Wow! Yes, it seems like they are getting a great deal as they know a lighter always cost much more than fifteen cents.

But in reality, the cheap lighters that we all sell in our stores usually coast us around six to nine cents each depending on who you buy it from. This kind of promotion can get your customers excited, not only that, but you will also save money doing it. Try it.

ONLINE AND SOCIAL MEDIA MARKETING

Now let's talk about online marketing. As I said, most big retailers spend two to three times more money on online advertising than they do on local area marketing expenses. Online promotions can be very creative. It can start from creating your website and having a strong web presence to dominating all parts of social media. But for now, for you to get started in online marketing, I don't think you need to jump all that high yet. Try some of the simpler and effective tricks which won't cost you anything.

Online marketing can be a broad area and topic. It can mean a thousand different things, but today we will only focus on the social media part of online marketing. Social media is the new buzz word for sites where people interact and share everything from quick thoughts to pictures to videos online in real time. I am sure you all know that, and the most popular social media sites lately are of course

Facebook, being number one, then there is Twitter, Pinterest, LinkedIn, and so many others. But for most brick and mortar retail businesses, in my opinion, the best and least expensive promotion you can run is by using social media marketing strategies and email marketing.

During the past few years, social media has taken marketing by storm. Every business has jumped on the bandwagon because that's where most of the consumers are. If a business does not have a web presence today, it simply does not exist, at least not for the millions of possible consumers that spend most of their time online. Social media provides a relatively inexpensive way to build relationships with customers which is very important in today's world. Without maintaining a good relationship with the customers, a business simply cannot grow.

Even retailers understand that a web presence is crucial today. Customers don't necessarily want to be able to purchase from you online, but they like to know more about you. Customers want a connection which is possible through social media. Social channels help a business project a favorable and positive image of themselves and drive more traffic to their website. Whether the intent is to cause awareness, obtain information, or sell items, a large number of consumers of any business are online, effectively navigating their way through the amount of information available online.

Today, social media marketing has become an integral part of any company's marketing strategy and for a good reason. A web presence has become necessary for most companies as they realize the significant chunk of consumers is now online. With the shifting preferences of consumers and Internet penetration driving consumer purchase behavior, they prefer using online channels to make their purchasing decisions.

Communication channels have also shifted online with consumers preferring online modes of communication with a brand. Consumers today don't prefer calling the store or writing to them. Instead, they prefer using the social media profile in the case of concerns and queries. Posting information publicly is another thing which businesses have to deal with. Along with social media marketing, online reputation management becomes necessary. If your business is not active online, but your consumer market is, you won't know what they are saying about you or even if they know about you.

Having a brick and mortar store is one thing, but promoting it is very different. For this, a retail business owner must know their customer profile thoroughly. There may be some consumers you can reach without any marketing, but there are many others which may be very active online and don't pay much heed to stores otherwise. By engaging those online customers, a business can ensure that they are spreading the word about their business and effectively opening communication channels to connect.

Customers like to know their brands today. This is very different from a few years ago when customers weren't bothered much about business. They were only interested in buying the product and understanding information which was fed to them. The changing times have changed the consumer mindset, and today, only those businesses succeed who can form positive relationships with their target audience.

HOW CAN YOU IMPROVE YOUR SOCIAL INFLUENCE?

Social media marketing brings results but with constant effort. When you are online making connections, spreading the word is a slow process. This also means ensuring that the right channels are used effectively. As a retail store business owner, you must start with finding out where the majority of your consumers lie. For instance, if the majority of your customers are active on Twitter but you are more active on Facebook, it won't produce the desired results. Using the right tools on the right websites is necessary.

As a retailer, you can also increase your social media influence by connecting with influencers in your industry. Influencers are bloggers who already have a following of online consumers who look up to them. Partnering with such influencers can give a retailer access to a large audience who are already used to buying similar products. Since they look up to the blogger, the chances are more likely that if you get an endorsement from industry influencers, you will gain access to those consumers as well.

Consumers are more likely to try your product or services when it is endorsed by someone who they look up to. Using this strategy can help retailers increase their sales and boost their profit in a relatively short time.

As a retailer, you can make use of the current happenings in the area you operate, as well as globally, to spread your message and connect with consumers online. A retailer must understand that no matter how useful and important social media marketing is for the business; it brings slow results. It can't be used immediately as a way to make sales, but it should be an integral part of the marketing strategy to form a relationship with the online consumer and spread awareness. Awareness is the first step to making sales.

Another way that retailers can use social media marketing to boost their sales and profits is by using their website to help customers. A consumer may be smart in making decisions, but the entire purchase cycle is based on a complex buying behavior. In your store alone, the consumer can get confused about where to go and which kinds of products to buy. If it's an online store, it is crucial to make navigation easier for the customer to find their way, the products they want, adding those products to their cart, and checkout. Retailers can become favorable by being available and making it easier for them when it comes to making the decision by providing them with value-laden information.

There are many ways in which consumers can be reached to provide them with information to help make their purchase decision easier such as retail store operators who can use the website to make product suggestions, promote customer reviews, advice customers on their popular and best-selling items, and to create awareness of special deals.

Social communities have risen in power, and a retailer who's online or offline cannot afford one bad review about them. There are websites and services, rating and ranking products, and if you get on their radar chances are your customers will step back from engaging with you.

So as much as creating a positive social media awareness and marketing is important, so is enhancing service standards. Depending on the kind of product or service a retailer sells, they can create social media communities and invite their consumers to participate and interact in a favorable environment. When customers feel like a community where they can discuss and share their concerns, it creates a positive image and an effective way for a company to paint themselves in a positive light.

Social media is one of the best ways to interact. Open the channels of communication with customers and give them a feel for your brand. It helps nurture relationships with customers which otherwise could be difficult to do on an ongoing basis such as in a brick and mortar store. If you're not online and only operating from a store using traditional marketing, it does not give you the opportunity to engage in meaningful communication with the customer.

You can only interact with them when they drop by the store, or through your marketing message. However, if you're using a website, you can get personal with your customer and give them incentives to engage with you. In today's world, the consumer has the power, and you can't simply expect them to walk in and become your customer.

Before entering into a relationship with any retail store, the consumer wants to know them, their vision and strategy, showing their marketing messages, and in need of a value-laden exchange of information before they are willing to part with their hard earned money.

Running effective social media campaigns can ensure that a retail store owner projects a positive image of themselves, connect with their online consumers, and increase their brand awareness. Not only for retail stores, but social media also is an effective way for customers to communicate with their favorite brand. On the one hand, where retailers can use it to increase awareness and communication, it also gives the customers a chance to project a positive business image. If you have dealt with your customers favorably in store, they are most likely to go online and give a business a positive review.

Studies show that any online customer is more influenced by a positive social review or through their peers who report a positive business experience.

HOW TO USE THE FIVE BIG WEBSITES TO DRIVE SOCIAL MEDIA INFLUENCE

Business needs to be active on social media to reach a wider audience. However, when it comes down to the actual task, it may not be that easy. Businesses can feel like they are running out of ideas to engage their audience through social media.

As much as social media marketing helps to promote the brand, it also helps to learn more about the customer, their demands, and needs. Here are some ways a retail store can use the five big websites to engage online consumers and promote sales.

FACEBOOK

Facebook isn't just a social media tool; it has become significant regarding advertising and marketing. Facebook allows businesses to have their own business page and compile data through Facebook Insights. Using this, retailers can compare their social media traffic and enhance their sales.

Facebook is one of the leading websites to promote your store with the help of blogs and brand related information. A retailer must be able to provide valuable information to form a connection and get more shares and likes to position yourself as a favorable brand on Facebook. You can also post questions which are very effective ways to learn what customers want to see in your store, and what they are most likely to purchase. It's like conducting a focus group online, only much easier and efficient as your customers become engaged.

Here is a great idea I tried in my store on Facebook. Create a business page for your store, and then print out some something like "Add us as your friend on Facebook and get a $1 off coupon." Then give your Facebook address. You can print eight to ten of these on one 8"x11" piece of paper, then cut them in pieces and have an employee pre-stuff them in shopping bags that you use at your store.

When I did this the first time, I spent about $475 or so the first month in coupons, but I gained access to the exact number of customers too. The next month, I started to send some specials that I ran on soda and many other items and saw my sales increase by about 9% the following month. It works, trust me, go try it and you will be amazed how well this works and how simple this can be.

Remember not to overdo it, or send specials once and then forget all about it until next year. Keep it consistent, maybe one a month or so is a great frequency, but if you want to be a little more aggressive, go twice a month.

TWITTER

Tweet chats allow a way for a retailer to engage the customers and show them that they are interested in listening to their opinions. It can also help identify influencers and engage with them. Tweet chats can also help gather consumer insights.

It could be used as an effective way to gather data by conducting a poll, engaging in trending conversations, and position the brand as favorable. Twitter can also be used to entice customers, engage in friendly jokes, and talk about products in a funny way to generate buzz.

TUMBLR

Retailers can use Tumblr in more or less the same way as other websites. However, it provides page customization about the vision and brand of the business. There is no limitation of character count or design on Tumblr or blogs in general, which help develop the right business image you want to produce.

Blogs are an excellent way to engage with the audience with relevant information and give incentive to the customer by creating meaningful content in the form of videos, eBooks, and articles.

INSTAGRAM AND PINTEREST

Pinterest and Instagram have increased in popularity as a means for advertising and marketing for brands. It allows retailers to show fascinating pictures of their products, give sneak peeks of new products, create a video marketing presentation, and show behind the scenes photos of an elaborate marketing campaign.

Customers today love knowing more about brands and behind the scenes gives the perfect way to connect. Visual engagement has become increasingly popular and is a good way to get views and create awareness. Aesthetically pleasing images are more shareable as well as generate more buzz. Businesses can effectively engage their target audience by sharing the relevant images and promoting them through   hashtags.

```
Name:

_____

Email Address:

_____

Born Before 1996?  Y      N

        (Please Circle)

    We will email you special
```

EMAIL

Make some small templates like the one in the image and ask your employees to have customers fill them out. I assure you in just two weeks you will have over 300 in your email list that you can directly market your store to. One word of advice, don't overdo it, do not send them an email every week or every day, but do it only when you have some real savings and promotions for them.

For example, your Coke or Pepsi 2-liter bottles are going on sale next week for a whole month, send them an email notifying them of that sale along with two other sales. Try to have at least three different sales in one email, and try to send one every month. Again, not every week.

Now let's talk about how to send these emails. There are a couple of email marketing companies that you can sign up with, and if you have less than one thousand subscribers, you can use them for free, meaning absolutely no cost to you.

One is MailChimp; I personally use their service, and it is free. Go to mailchimp.com and sign up for a free account and then take their guided video tour and see how simple it is to send hundreds or even thousands of people one email just by clicking a button.

4. STREAMLINING COSTS AND EXPENSES

It is worthwhile for retail store owners to keep up with the changes in the retail industry and adapt to them for better sales. From the store outlook to its product placement and other things, it can make a big difference for you to pay some attention to details.

When it comes to streamlining business costs and expenses, most retailer store operators are overlooking simple facts that may enhance their store's outlook. From your store location to the kind of products that you stock and how you operate it, everything matters.

Many store operators ignore upgrades and minimal changes that could elevate the look of your store and instead, only focus on making sales. What you have to understand is that if you're not going to put money into your business, you are not going to reap a lot back from it. There are many things if you pay close attention, to what could help you enhance your sales by streamlining your costs and expenses.

There are necessary expenses to be made such as those required to upgrade the store. Most retail store owners don't put money into fixing their lights, changing their displays, cleaning dust off shelves every day, and in the end, complain about high operating costs versus low profits. If you are not going to give your customer a good shopping experience, no matter how big or small, your store will not be able to generate sales.

It is crucial to learn how to manage your money and cut down on unnecessary expenses. The very first place to start, if you want to streamline your costs and expenses, is the bank. Most people don't pay attention to how much they are paying the bank in extra service charges every month, and that could be causing a big dent on your profit and loss statement.

Obtain your bank analysis statement which has a breakdown of your basic service charges, and study them carefully to find out where you can cut down. Do you necessarily require all the listed services, or you can do without some of them? Talk to your banker if you need to understand how you can reduce your bank costs.

Another thing is to invest in a sophisticated accounting system and save yourself the trouble later on. If you are not evaluating your costs and expenses on an automated system, it is unlikely that you will be efficient with your money. Companies that don't invest in a good accounting software face difficulty at tax or audit time.

If you are a growing retail company, you must be able to decipher where you stand among your competition. Your company should have some industry benchmarks to evaluate its costs and expenses to understand where you may be underspending or overspending. Such industry data and statistics are available, but most companies don't think of making use of it. It's critical data at your disposal which can help you streamline your costs and expenses.

Before a formal audit takes place, which is for entirely different reasons, you must conduct an internal audit and review your revenue. Studying the incoming and outgoing revenue carefully can help highlight costs that are too high, areas where your business has dipped in revenue, and other costs that can be controlled. Operating costs are another thing that a business can streamline. Are you using an energy efficient heating system or is there a way you can cut your utility costs? Sometimes a company is spending too much on travel costs, or there are some aspects of the job that could be done at home or online. Consider all these possibilities to minimize your operating costs.

The success of a retail store depends on the efficiency of its stocking. Understand your inventory cost and time, and see if you can cut back on it. Improve your stocking efficiency by satisfying customer demand with just as many products that you know will sell as opposed to having an inventory of goods.

You can't possibly streamline your costs and expenses unless and until you regularly evaluate them. There are some expenses, which are necessary to undertake to make your retail store more efficient and effective. Continuous assessment will help you recognize the unnecessary costs which your store might be taking on and instead invest money in necessary expenses that will help give it a boost.

Where your store is located is another factor that helps you grow, because it is vital to target the demographics of the location you are operating in. Some items may be popular in other locations but not at yours. What you need to do is stock things which your demographic market is interested in purchasing, and then streamlining the process so that it takes minimal time to restock.

There are three primary ways we can make our business lean, mean, and a great money making machine. First, by reducing operating costs or expenses, second, by negotiating and finding the right vendors to buy from, and lastly, by reducing theft and employee errors. Now let's talk about some real life examples so you can understand and relate, as we will talk real numbers from my own business.

I recently made a few rather simple changes in operating expenses and picked up an extra $1,700 a month. Well, it's not too good to be true, so just stay with me here. We all are in business to do what? Make $$$, right? How do we go about making that money? By selling products and services from our store. The more we sell, the more we make, and the less we sell, the less we make.

I am sure you all will agree with me so far. Now we all also know that sales don't go up or increase overnight. As I mentioned earlier, that with the right marketing tips and tricks, you could slowly increase sales. But saving money on your everyday operating costs is always a sweet added bonus, and for this, you don't actually have to work that hard. When you save money on your operational expenses, it goes directly to your bottom line profit. I will go through a checklist here, so it is easier for everyone to keep track of it.

First, let's define operating expenses or costs before we go any further. Now there are two types of operating costs and expenses:

1. Fixed Costs or Expenses
2. Variable Costs or Expenses

Fixed costs are exactly what the name says, they are fixed, and they don't change month to month or by how much your sales grow. Your rent, insurance, and property taxes are fixed. More simply, the costs that are not related or associated with your sales are usually fixed. Meaning, if you do any business or not, your rent still has to be paid. So are your property taxes and insurance.

But the variable costs are the ones that are usually somewhat related to your sales, like labor cost. The more business you do, the more people you will need to hire, so it is directly related to your sales. On the other hand, if your store is closed, then you have no employees working, so no labor cost.

I know your rent, and other fixed costs are not something we can touch or shrink so let's not worry about it. It's not like we can go to the landlord or the bank and say, "Hey, I am trying to cut down on operating expenses, can you reduce my rent by $1,000 a month, please?" That won't go very well, so don't try that. Instead, let's try to save on the expenses and see what we can do. Here are some of the variable costs or expenses we all pay every month:

- Power
- Water
- Natural Gas
- Garbage/Trash removal
- Phone/Internet
- Janitorial service

These are also the expenses that can take the majority of your savings, and that is what we will be talking about. First, let me share a case study of one of my own stores and how we saved over $1,500 each month. Here are all the utility bills for that store for this past June:

1. Power bill - $2,665
2. Water bill - $477
3. Natural gas - $567
4. Garbage service - $235
5. Janitorial and towel service - $125 (the reason it is a little high, is because we have a deli in this store, so we use a lot of towels that also come from the same janitorial company)
6. Phone and Internet - $173

I went back and looked at my bills for the same month of the previous year, and this is what they were:

1. Power bill - $3,933
2. Water bill - $621
3. Natural gas bill - $726
4. Garbage/trash bill - $297

5. Janitorial services - $125
6. Phone and Internet - $289

I know it is hard to remember all these numbers but let me add both of these up for you. Last year our total utility bills were $5,991. This June, the total bill was $4,242. The difference between last June and this June was exactly $1,749. That's the money we saved in one month compared to the same month last year. Let me explain how we made that change, and reduced these utility bills.

I will tell you what we did in this store was a little too much, and you may not want to make all the changes we did; as we spent, I think, it was a little over $6,500 to achieve these savings, but to me, that was money well spent. Okay, let me first explain what we did.

This store is about 3,500 square feet and has a decent size deli restaurant in it. As you can imagine, anytime a store has a deli, the utility costs usually go up because of all the cooking equipment that run every day, not to mention all the heat those machines and display cases produce.

Our first target was to reduce the power/electricity bill, as that is the biggest of all the bills. First, we looked at the lighting inside and outside the store. As for the inside lights, we had 42 typical fluorescent light fixtures, and each of those fixtures had four 48-inch bulbs, and each bulb is around 40 watts. So each fixture is consuming 160 watts of power.

Ninety percent of the commercial facilities have these types of light fixtures. I searched and found a local LED light supplier who sources directly from China, and I bought one hundred 48-inch LED bulbs. These bulbs look exactly like the fluorescent ones and fit the same way in the existing fixtures, but they are LED inside, so they only burn about 10-12 watts of power. But they put out much brighter lights.

Now, in those 42 fixtures, each had four bulbs in it, so all together we had 168 bulbs, but I bought only 100 because the supplier showed us we should only put two bulbs in each fixture and not four, as that would be overkill since just two LED bulbs can produce more light than four of those old fluorescents could do.

I hired an electrician, and all he had to do is bypass the ballast on each of those fixtures and install two bulbs on each. It took him four hours, and I paid him $350 to get it all done. What I did here is most fixtures have two bulbs, but only a handful has four. I wanted some areas to be brighter than others. Areas like right on top of the cooler doors, over the deli case, the coffee area, and around the checkout counter.

This way I created some highlights inside the store. Now let's see what we changed regarding wattage so far. We had 168 bulbs, and each was 40 watts if I add all those wattages of all the old bulbs, we were using 6,720 watts, and now we are using 1,200 watts. The difference is 5,520 watts, so we reduced the consumption by one-fifth of what it used to be. I forgot to mention that I paid right around $12 for each bulb. I was surprised to see the difference in brightness at night inside the store; it simply looked beautiful. Like the store had a nice makeover.

On the outside canopy, we had 14 big light fixtures (like most gas station canopies have), and I think they each use 450 watts of power. The supplier offered me those canopy lights for $325; each only uses 100 watts of power and my electrician offered to install each for $45. So to get them replaced, it would cost $5,180. I took the plunge and told them to go ahead and do it.

I had two motives for deciding to do this. First, of course, huge savings on the power bill, and second, the improvement on appearance, especially at night. I am sure you all have seen some of the new gas stations or other businesses with all LED lights inside and out, and how beautiful and shiny they all look.

After all the work was done, in total we spent $6,730 and achieved two things. Good savings and a brighter and shinier look. Though I knew we would be saving money, I wasn't sure just how much until I got the power bill the following month. I was under the impression that since I reduced the wattage consumption by one-fifth (in my naive mind), I was hoping I would see my power bill go down by the same ratio, but I was wrong!

It went down about $900 or so each month, on the average. To be honest, I was a little disappointed, but

I figured I would make the investment back in about eight months, and after the eighth month, it will be a savings of $900 each month which is not bad. I was happy that we got the brighter look, and we have been getting a lot of compliments too.

Around the same time, we had to get some A/C work done by a company who, after finishing their work, made some recommendations based on his observations. I listened carefully. He suggested if I make a few changes, I would see significant savings on my power bill and as I was on a roll to save money. I told him to get the work done. This is what he suggested:

1. Use a lock box for both A/C thermostats, so no one can alter the temperature (we noticed employees, and sometimes customers were putting the thermostat down to 62 degrees which, in the summertime, an AC will not reach. Instead it will freeze up)
2. Change my A/C filters every two weeks in the summer and every month in the winter (he explained, since we do a lot of cooking, the grease gets into the air and clogs the filter faster than in any other non-cooking stores)
3. Clean and wash the vent hood filters on top of the fryers every week
4. Add two thermostat controlled attic exhaust fans
5. Add two good quality pedestal fans in the kitchen and behind the counter, so the air will

move and circulate better and make the store feel cooler.

The cost was mostly to add two fans to the attic which was around $850. Altogether his bill was around $1,000. But after we implemented these changes, I did see my power bill go down by about another $400. Now I am sure you will agree to spend $1,000 one-time to save $400 each month is a great deal. If you don't want to spend the money on the LED conversion now, don't, instead make these small changes and see a difference next month.

Next, I called my handyman; I am sure if you are in the gas station business, you too, have a guy that can do a lot of minor repair work. I had him change all the faucets in the store to auto shut off faucets (bought them from Amazon). I also had him change the flush on the toilets to the water saving flush system. If you recall, my water bill from last year to this year went down by $144. That is a saving of $1,700 every year.

Then I looked at our phone bills, and with Internet and three phone lines, we were paying almost $300 a month. I took a deal from the local cable company and bought their Internet for $55 a month and had AT&T drop their Internet service and went from three phones lines to just two. The bill from AT&T is now around $118 a month, so by changing the service, we are now saving $127 each month. Not bad, huh?

Next, I had both water heaters checked for temp setting and found out both were set around 145 degrees. The local health department only requires it to be around 120 degrees, and since both of the water heaters run on gas, just by adjusting the temperature, our natural gas bill dropped by $159. Again, not bad.

Lastly, I observed our trash/dumpster service and noticed since we do a lot of cooking in our deli. Naturally we produce a lot of trash. We had two 6-yard containers that get picked up once a week. I called around and found a company that offered me one 8-yard container with twice a week pickup for $235 which is $62 less than what I was paying. But there was one extra benefit to having your trash picked up twice a week I didn't know at the time. The flies, bugs and bad odors around the dumpster outside were gone.

Now let's recap:

> Savings from LED light conversions is around $900 each month.
> Savings from attic vent fans and lockbox is $400 each month.
> Savings from water bill is $144 each month.
> Savings from the phone and the Internet is $116 each month.
> Savings from the natural gas bill is $159 each month.
> And lastly, savings from changing the dumpster service is $62 each month.

All total for the month of June this year it was $1,749 savings compared to last June. If you are feeling motivated and want to try some changes, then my suggestion is you do the following:

1. Get your handyman to check all the doors to see if there are gaps, if there are, have him close them as cold air leaks out, and hot air gets in through any doors and windows that are not properly closing.
2. Check your faucets and bathroom flush system, see if there are water leaks, also decide if you want to change to auto shut off faucets or not.
3. Check your water heater temperature setting.
4. Check your attic if you have one, and make sure you have enough exhaust and ventilation there, if not install some fans.
5. Add lock boxes to your A/C thermostat and set them at 74 or 75 degrees depending on where you are located.
6. Add pedestal fans to circulate air.
7. Set reminders in your phone to replace A/C filters every two weeks in the summer.
8. Ask an electrician if they can install a timer/sensor for your outside and canopy lighting, so they come on at a set time every day and go off at a set time every day so there is no room for error.
9. Look through your phone bills, trash pickup service bills, and call some of their competitors and see what they are offering.

10. Lastly, if you can afford to spend the money go for all LED conversion if not get just the inside of the store done which is not a lot of money and you make that back in just a few months.

Now if these ten items each can save you $100 average, you will, at least, save $1000 a month, now it is up to you to go and try it.

One word of caution, you may find LED bulbs that cost a fraction of what I said I paid but remember not all bulbs are created equal, sometimes you get what you pay for. Be careful and buy only from reputable companies. Cheap LED lights can lose their brightness in just about a year, do some research before buying.

VENDOR NEGOTIATION

For you to grow your retail business, it is important to conduct productive vendor negotiations to get the best possible rates/prices on your purchased items. For this, you need to be aware of the current price rate in the market, review the trends, and study the market conditions before getting into negotiations with your vendor. Remember you will only be as effective as your communication skills because the vendor will try to maximize their profit while you have to maximize yours. Here are some ways to conduct negotiations with vendors.

RENEGOTIATE ANNUALLY

Multiyear contracts are not in your favor, and it is a much better policy to renegotiate your vendor agreements each year. It is most likely to result in lower costs as the annual bidding forces the vendors to reconsider and change their rate as prices may have fluctuated.

It is never a good idea to go into negotiations or renegotiations without adequate preparation, and if you don't, you will most likely end up defeated by your vendor. It is also a good idea to check rates with multiple vendors before choosing one even when its renegotiations, and let them know you have quotes from multiple vendors. This essentially creates competitive pricing which gives you the leverage.

UNDERTAKE REGULAR SPENDING ASSESSMENTS

Today's business environment is very budget conscious, and if you write out purchase orders waiting for suppliers to fulfill their commitment at an affordable price, then you may be in for a surprise. It is not the way to do business and certainly not if you want to obtain the best rates.

Take control of the situation and analyze how much you regularly spend on specific vendors. You should be able to deduce how much you are spending and what you are getting in return. By doing an assessment on multiple vendors, you will get an idea of the prices for similar goods other vendors are selling and their services.

It will also help you understand the potential of negotiating points and how much you are spending over time. As you conduct regular spending assessments, you will learn where you are spending the most money and how you can bring down vendor costs. By studying this data, a company can also obtain volume discounts, especially if it sees that its different businesses in different locations are obtaining the same things at different rates.

EXPLORE ALTERNATIVES

Sometimes companies become set in their vendor negotiations. If you're purchasing something from one vendor for the past ten years, it may be that you have stopped looking for other alternatives to cut costs. Because the vendor rapport and pricing has become something that your company is used to and information relationships have become part of business, it may be difficult to break free of them. However, if not in five years, things have changed considerably; it is very likely that you can obtain the same thing at half the price from somewhere else. Unless you research your alternatives, you wouldn't find out about it and remain unable to maximize profits.

DO YOUR HOMEWORK

Apart from having complete information about pricing so that you can craft your argument effectively, it is also essential that you obtain some information from prospective suppliers from their customers. Any supplier you are considering entering into a contract with shouldn't mind sharing their customer list with you, because if they are serving and satisfying other customers, why not you?

Customers are very likely to talk about their vendor relationships, especially about the products they purchase from them which they like and which they don't. If you approach them correctly, they may even share their prices with you, which is very much in your favor. It will ensure that your vendor doesn't quote you a higher rate, and even if they do, you can negotiate it with them.

BE AWARE OF PRICE CREEP

If you're not doing your homework and don't know what costs are currently prevailing in the market, it is very likely that you will fall prey to price creep. When your supplier knows that you don't keep a check on prices, they are very likely to charge you any price, and since you do not know the price, you are likely to comply.

This is something, which prevents business growth and goes unnoticed and unspotted for a long while. When your vendor knows that you keep track of prices, they can't overcharge you. This also ensures that as prices climb up, you are not ripped off. Your vendor will still be mindful of charging you reasonable rates.

As a business, you need to understand and keep in mind that with today's technological advancements and other factors playing a key role in vendor success, the power has shifted from the buyer to the supplier. Vendors may have eliminated competitors by driving prices too low, or the fast growing demand has prompted the transition of power.

Buyers can't afford to be in a weak position with their vendor because then you wouldn't be able to negotiate skillfully. In such case, a buyer needs to approach the situation strategically. If you have to negotiate with a powerful vendor here is how you should proceed.

PROVIDE VALUE

There is always some kind of value that you can bring to your supplier to negotiate a price decrease with them. Suppose, if you are stuck in a situation where you have to pay your vendor high prices because of any reason, and you know they are trying to enter a new market where you are also entering. It may be difficult for them to enter but it's not for you.

You can offer to give them a foothold in the new market in exchange for a price reduction. This is an example of an irresistible offer with the aspect of a win-win situation.

REDUCE THEIR RISK

Another way to negotiate with a powerful vendor is to contribute to reducing their price risk. As a retail store owner, if you can give your vendor a value proposition in any way, which can benefit them, chances are, in return you can request a reduced rate.

When the vendor will benefit from the deal so will they have to pass the benefit to you as well. Only in this way, the power of vendors can be broken. No matter what difficult situation you are stuck in, using your resources and influence can always help overcome any adverse situation and negotiate with vendors favorably.

When you are dealing with a tough vendor who isn't willing to budge on their prices or you don't have an alternate solution to it, some companies resort to canceling all deals with the current vendor. Although this is a risky strategy to undertake, and can put your business at risk but can be used as a last resort. If you have been a major customer for the vendor and all of a sudden you decide to terminate all deals with them, it means a big business loss for the vendor. This could lead them to agree to your reduced price rates. However, as mentioned earlier, this is a risky approach that a business only takes as a last resort.

5. MINIMIZING THEFT AND ERRORS

Typically, most large retailers set aside a budget of around 1%-2% of total sales which they call "retail loss." It is a huge number and hard to comprehend, but often, most small and large retailers end up losing around 1%-2% of their total sales in theft by both customers and by employees, by errors, mishandling of inventory, and various errors.

As a small business owner, if you pay attention, and keep your eyes on just a few things, you can save more money and make your business run lean and mean and find more efficient ways to make more money. Again these are additional savings to you but more importantly, it is vital that you follow through since it is all about theft. Remember, regardless of how well your merchandising or pricing is, if people are stealing from you, chances are you won't see much of profit or results from all your good work.

It is hard to stop theft completely. If we want to be realistic, we should try to control theft and not try to eliminate it all the way, which some of you may disagree with, but remember, as long as you have employees, there will be a certain degree of soft and hard theft. I will explain what those two are in a minute. But in my twenty plus years of experience, I have seen it is quite impossible to eliminate theft completely unless you want to sacrifice your home, family, and social life and stand behind your employees all day and night.

My point is as long as you can cut down and minimize theft into a more manageable fashion, you should be okay. I remember when I went to dealer training school up in Cleveland years ago, one of the instructors from BP corporate told us they had accepted a 2% retail loss for each and every store they operate. Meaning, they accepted that they would lose 2% inventory, money, or other assets, and as long as they can keep it under that 2%, they consider that a success. At that time, I didn't agree with them but found out later that yes, if you can keep your losses within 1%-1.5%, you are doing great.

Okay, let me first explain and define theft. Theft occurs in two different ways in most businesses.

➢ External
➢ Internal

EXTERNAL THEFT

External theft is what the name says; it is external, meaning it happens by people from outside, more precisely, external theft is when your customers and vendors are stealing from you. Every store has some degree of external theft, let's face it, one out of ten customers will pocket a pack of gum or a small candy bar, and there is not much you can do about it. It happens every day. While it will be a challenge to stop it all the way, you can deter theft by taking a few measures. It is a 3 step process.

➢ Detect
➢ Deter
➢ Defend

For external theft, as I said, happens in two ways, by your customers, and by your vendors. First, you need to identify where and how these thefts are taking place. Customers usually will pocket smaller items that typically cost over a $1. Your candy aisles, medicine, and health and beauty aisles are prime targets for them. Identify some of your merchandise that you think can be stolen easily, then try to arrange your store's layout in such a way that those aisles become very visible or close to the checkout counter where your employees can keep an eye on them.

To further deter and defend you can focus some of your surveillance cameras over those areas and install a video monitor where both your customers and cashiers can see them.

Remember, when a thief can see him or herself on the monitor, they get self-conscious, and that can be a good theft deterrent. Next, you can put a sign next to your front door where it says, "For customer's safety our premise is under 24-hour video surveillance." Usually, no one pays attention to this type of sign other than your occasional adventure seeking immature thieves. Next, you can add some theft deterrent convex mirrors around the back of your store that you can focus on the corners. They are typically not very expensive.

If your business is in the vicinity of a school, and you know you get a ton of kids coming into your store at a set time, limit how many kids can enter your store at one time.

Train your employees to make eye contact with every customer that walks through your front door. Studies have shown that if you make eye contact with a potential perpetrator or thief, that person will think twice before doing something wrong because, in their mind, they have been "Seen" by the employees. Let's recap how to detect, deter, and defend customer theft.

1. Identify merchandise that can be easily stolen
2. Change your layout where those types of merchandise can be better monitored
3. Focus your video cameras to watch those weak areas
4. Install a video monitor where both your cashiers and customers can see them
5. Put a sign in the front window about video surveillance
6. Install two theft deterrent convex mirrors around the back of your store
7. Limit how many kids can enter the store at one time (only if you are in a school zone)
8. Train employees to make eye contact with customers as soon as they walk in

The second part of external theft is the theft that happens by your vendors; now this is where you lose a lot more money compared to what you may lose by customer theft. Vendor theft happens mostly when they bring merchandise to the store and get checked in. If you've ever checked in any vendors, then you know they count fast and in increments of three, five, or even ten. So they may count here is 3, 6. 9, 12 or 10, 20, 30, 40 and so on. If you are not fast in counting, it can be hard to keep track of their counting style.

Some vendors can get very innovative when stealing; I remember years ago one of my soft drink vendors was stealing from me for months until one day when I happened to walk in as he was being checked in, and I caught him. He was bringing in ten cases of 20-ounce soda bottles in each load, and other than the very top case every case underneath was missing eight to ten bottles in the middle. From the outside, each crate looked full, but in the middle, they were each empty. The trick was, as soon as the cashier checked him in, he went into the cooler and acted like he was filling the shelves.

He would refill the missing bottles from other cases and eventually end up with two to three empty crates which we would think were empty because the products were on the shelves. That day, what happened was, I was missing a particular flavor of soda, and as they were counting, I lifted the top case to see if that flavor was underneath, as soon as I did that he panicked and tried to stop me. Without knowing, I lifted the case and saw the missing bottles in the middle! Things went downhill from there, I called his supervisor and had him leave the store immediately.

Anyway, long story short, the company issued me credit for 120 cases of products which they estimated he stole from us in the previous four months.

Now to detect, deter, and defend vendor theft, always make sure they are checked by you or your employees, but they have to take their time to check each and every item. Some stores have rules for vendors like no delivery after 4 pm (set a time when you or your manager leave for the day and make that the cutoff time).

If you have a deli and get busy during the lunch rush, inform vendors not to show up between 12:00-1:30 pm. Also, when checking in, make sure the products they are bringing in are not damaged.

INTERNAL THEFT

Now let's talk internal theft. I saved the best or worse, in this case, for last. Let's say you lose $1,000 a month; you can safely assume that 70%-80% of that theft took place internally or by your employees. Every dollar you lose due to theft, twenty cents of that was done by outsiders, and eighty cents was done by your own people. If gone undetected, theft can be like a plague, once infected it grows out of control quickly.

The reason it grows fast, I found out, is the simple psychology of people's thinking process. Let's say one of your employees stole $20 one day, and no one noticed. Next time, they work they will try to take $40. In their mind they feel the thrill of not being caught, it is like having an adrenaline rush, so the greed grows, and the amount grows bigger each time. Seldom have you found a smart thief who would only steal $20 each time they work and be satisfied. But if you have a thief like that, it is very hard to catch them. Employee theft can be broken down into two categories.

➢ Hard theft
➢ Soft theft

Let's take a look at how an employee can steal, what are our weak points in this line of business.

> - Doing refunds and voids
> - Not ringing up a sale
> - Doing "sweetheart" deals
> - Consuming or taking products for their own use
> - Taking merchandise home
> - Being short on their shift paperwork
> - "Riding the clock."

Now to set up a good defense against all this, first, let's define what products are more commonly stolen from gas stations by employees. In my experience, the top three categories are cigarettes, beer, and deli food, as they are high dollar items and more commonly bought, so they are also easy to steal.

To safeguard against theft you should always have a cigarette inventory count in every shift, where they do an IN count and an OUT count and see how many packs they sold during their shift, and they have to match that with their register sales.

Next is beer; it's a good idea to do a weekly inventory and count all the beer in retail and add all deliveries that come through the door and subtract all your weekly beer sales and see if that matches or comes close to the number you have on hand.

The deli is a tricky one; it is hard to catch since we typically sell so many varieties of food and meat. But I still use a daily inventory sheet that I ask my deli person to fill in every day, where I keep track of few key items. It is not a full proof system but a real deterrent as long as you keep an eye on that inventory sheet and spot check that at least once or twice a week. Let's recap on how we can deter and defend employee theft.

- ➢ Video surveillance (Only works if you watch from time to time)
- ➢ Cash register to video interface where all transactions get recorded
- ➢ Good hiring and background check process
- ➢ Having a functional inventory control system in place
- ➢ Periodic employee coaching and training
- ➢ Enforcing and monitoring clock in and out

Here is the calculation, say you sell $80,000 of merchandise a month from your store, if you lose 2% of your sales by theft each month, then $1,600 is what you are losing each month. Now that is a minimum; some stores lose much more than that. We also lose a lot of money by various errors especially by our employees; here is a list of mistakes.

- ➢ Charging the customer the wrong price, typically lower than actual price
- ➢ Accepting damaged or expired products from vendors
- ➢ Giving out bigger portions of food or other products then they are supposed to (If you have a deli)
- ➢ Not ringing up all the sales or merchandise

- Drive offs (If you operate gas station)
- Leaving canopy or other light fixtures on during daytime
- Mishandling products and foods

Typically, most businesses will lose around 1% of their sales from all these errors and mishaps. Coaching and training your employees properly can minimize most of these items. So based on $80,000 in monthly sales, if you train and coach your employees correctly, you may reduce some of these errors and thus saving around $800 a month. Say your success rate is 50% in reducing both external and internal theft and all employee errors, your savings can then be $1,600 + $800 = $2,400/2 = $1,200. You can add another $1,000 each month to your bottom line just by following these simples steps.

Any company that wants to increase their sales and boosts their profits starts with projecting a positive company image to attract customers. Businesses understand that they can drive their sales by understanding their customer psyche and developing good relations with them.

However, as much as the image and marketing are important so is correcting the organization's internal affairs. If you want to succeed in generating higher profits, it is also important to control employee theft and errors. No business wants to believe that their employees may be engaged in stealing, but if there are discrepancies in sales numbers, chances are you may have a problem at hand which requires immediate action.

Any retail store that cannot commit to its employees in a positive way will not be able to drive employee loyalty. When you hire a person, it's important to align their objective with the company vision and ideal. Any discrepancy in the objectives can result in a disengaged employee who will not be as productive and thus contribute to company growth.

Businesses that care about their employees, provide them incentives, and show that they care for them are better able to engage them. An engaged employee is more likely to work for the progress of the company as opposed to working for its downfall. Companies today are starting to realize the importance of employee commitment and use techniques to motivate them. When you have to increase sales, you have to focus on empowering and strengthening your employees so that they are loyal and work for the growth of the company.

Employee theft and errors are a big business cost that most organizations either ignore or fail to figure out, which causes damage to the bottom line. When employees are not engaged and committed, they are more likely to make errors and steal from the company. However, what a retail store needs to do to eliminate errors and theft is first to hire the right employees, train them, and create employee loyalty. Organizations that can cultivate this loyalty see that no external factors are diminishing their bottom line profits.

ONE EMPLOYEE AT A TIME

Theft often takes place when a single employee is left in charge of the store with no camera or another person to keep an eye on them. It is recommended that a retailer should never station a single employee at the store at one time and at the least, employ two employees together to avoid and discourage theft.

It can also help to have a second employee witness any void purchases or refunds. However, always pairing the same employees together can also do harm as they can form a close friendship and decide to help each other out in negative ways. Thus, it is important for a retailer to keep rotating employees and avoid pairing close friends or acquaintances together.

INSTALL SURVEILLANCE

If your store still does not have a surveillance system, it is time to get one. When employees know that they are being watched or that any of their wrongdoings can be reported, they are less likely to engage in theft. It can pay off, in the long run, to have a high definition video surveillance system in the shop to keep a virtual eye on all employees working in the store. Retailers can also use an exception based reporting system at the point of sale to keep a check on employees. Using the system can help flag any fraudulent transaction in case of voids or refunds or release of excessive funds outside of store operating hours.

Retailers can effectively control employee theft using these techniques, but what about employee errors? Anyone is prone to making errors but what matters is that employees learn to correct them. For employees to not make errors and provide exceptional customer service to customers which motivate them to come back to the store or engage with the retailer online, training is imperative.

By identifying errors and training gaps, a retailer can ensure that the gap is minimized and thus errors, by providing the right guidance. Not everyone learns at the same pace, and not all the employees you hire will have the same experience level. Employees come from different backgrounds, have different learning capacities, and experience which is important to take into account when providing them training.

Errors can reflect directly on a store's sales and turn them negative. Too many errors can discourage the customer from opting for your store. It is important to keep a check on employees and address the training gaps as and when required, to avoid this from happening.

4 STEPS TO 25% SALES BOOST IN 60 DAYS

Now it's time to set up some specific goals that are attainable to get to the target sales in two months doing exactly what I just outlined earlier. This is how you will get there.

1. The first week you need to focus on your product line and merchandising efforts. Follow those steps, tweak and fix what you need to fix in your merchandising lineup. Every time I took over a new business, this is what I would do the very first week, where I go and remerchandise the store with the right type of products and place them where they belong.

Typically, just by remerchandising and bringing in more targeted products for that specific neighborhood. Week one, do your research about the neighborhood and identify your product lines that are well targeted towards your local market, then do a layout on a piece of paper of how you want the product displays to flow. Week two, you order the products, and in week three, you do the changes and all the actual remerchandising that you planned in the last two weeks.

In this same period, you can also implement everything that I mentioned under Pricing Strategy as well, remember, effective merchandising and effective pricing both go hand in hand and so you need to implement both at the same time. By doing this you will create a WOW factor in your store when customers walk in and see the new layout of your store, along with all the new products and it will only get better if you have great, and often times, lower prices to display on those products. Just these two changes alone can improve your sales by 5%-10%.

2. Next, you will need help from your employees. But before they can offer their help, you need to make sure you hire, train, coach, and empower them. Teach them the basics of Marketing 101 and make sure to reward them for the right behavior. Remember, it's all about motivation. If you follow the steps properly, you should see an increase in your sales by at least 5%, maybe much more. If you start this process the first week, this will take you three weeks or a little more to complete and a month to see the positive results.

3. Time to take a look at all the offline ways (event promotion, sponsoring the local school, church events, and games) I spoke about promoting your business. Remember those? If you try half of what we discussed, you should see an increase of 2%-5% in your business.

The biggest hike will, and should come from all the Internet or online efforts that you undertake. I have seen it first hand, and I know if you do things right like Facebook, collect email addresses, and all the other ideas, you should see an increase of at least 8%-10%.

So far, we have increased sales by at least 5% from item number one by implementing effective merchandising and pricing strategies. The second increase of 5% comes from your employees. The third increase originates from all offline and online marketing efforts. Both combined is, at least, a 10% boost.

5% + 5% + 10% = 20%

We have a little ways to go to get to our 25% sales boost goal. For this last 5%, we will have to take a different approach. Instead of boosting sales, we will reduce cost and expenses, so we end up with a savings that will translate into the same dollar value as if we increased sales by another 5%.

4. A. For this, we will take the measures I discussed on how to save on operating expenses, and reduce theft and errors, which should translate into, at the very least, a 3% savings overall and it should not take more than five weeks to implement and see a difference.

4. B. Lastly, you should sit down and negotiate with all your vendors and see how you can get better pricing from them either by changing vendors or by buying bigger volume. Typically, a good negotiation can result in savings of, at least, 2-3%. You can do this the very first or the second week and see some savings by the end of the second month, depending on how often you buy from them.

Did we get to our target of a 25% sales increase? Yes, we did, and as for getting there in 60 days, as you can see most of these changes you can implement simultaneously. But it may take a few weeks to see the final results. In my opinion, by the eighth week, you should be able to see all the positive results trickling down to your bank.

THE FUTURE OF RETAIL BUSINESS

I get asked this often from my readers; they often ask where is the future of retail heading to. As I tell them, there is no one-word answer to this question, but I know this as a retail business owner, if you want to thrive, you need to understand the problems and challenges associated with it as well as the future of retail sales. The advent of technology has changed many things and is driving a profound shift in all industries. As such, it is predicted that the retail sales business will also undergo immense pressure in all aspects of retail, which will further redefine the customer experience.

Brick and mortar stores no longer remain long enough to garner sales in this tough and competitive environment because of e-commerce penetration. It has become important for any kind of retail business to have an online presence and attract its customers in whatever way possible, as long as it's aligned with their business philosophy.

Having said that, technologies such as virtual reality and the Internet of Things are shaking things up in a big way. On the flip side, remember, when you are selling needed items like grocery, fuel, or similar items, the Internet will not be a competition to you. The Internet cannot fill up your tank, cut your hair, paint your toenails, or sell you a candy bar that you want to consume right now. Nor can it serve you fresh food, fruits, or drinks. It does depend on what product or services you sell out of your retail store.

Now let's look at some of the ways retail sales are predicted to change in the future.

ENHANCED REWARDS

Retailers are already pushing for consumer insights and data through their sign up forms, email newsletter, marketing surveys, and so on. Every minute that is being spent on a retail website, it is giving information and data on consumers and the target audience.

That pushes retailers to provide more customized and tailored solutions to its customers based on those insights. The future of this in retail could mean that consumers will expect more value-laden rewards from the company. Buyers just don't settle for purchase points, discounts, and other kinds of incentives any longer. The customer loyalty program will stretch beyond that. Customers expect more convenient services and non-purchase interactions as well.

CLIENT BUILDING

Retail has gone beyond just a mere customer-seller interaction. It has become a trustworthy relationship that extends beyond you selling an item and the other person purchasing it. Retailers are pushing to actually "know" their customers so that they can reach out to them in a personalized way. They need to form a trust with their customer for a recurring purchase and at the same time, reach out to new buyers and build trust. However, relationship building with customers is going a step further as retailers use technology, which will help them identify and establish personalized relationships with each shopper.

Retailers can enable a more helpful shopping experience by asking for particular and meaningful information and past purchase history to help create a unique shopping experience.

NAVIGATION PLANNING

The shopping experience and its impact on the shopper start to build as soon as the shopper steps foot into the store. Retailers will have to implement a changed and much more effective navigation process, which provides a smooth shopping experience. The navigation process is essentially built on assumptions which guide a shopper through the store. Retailers will go a step beyond to understand their navigation process and how it takes place to gauge what attracts buyers.

Things like how customers move through the aisles, react to products, and where they spend the more time matter the most when it comes to creating the navigation process which enhances the shopping experience and directs the buyer actually to make a purchase. Such insights can further help retailers make important decisions about traffic flow and promotion offerings.

THE VIRTUAL EXPERIENCE

Virtual reality is fast replacing the physical world and shopping, as we know it. Connectivity through wearable devices and smartphones is changing how we see the world around us, and this is going to affect the retail world largely. Shoppers will be able to gain access to complete information on products they like as they move through a store through augmented reality.

They will also be able to see how a particular dress looks without even wearing it. Virtual reality is going to change the retail world in a big way as consumers find it more convenient and easier to sift through virtual recommendations based on their body type, find out how they look in it without even trying it, and just walk to the counter to pick the product. All hassle seems to go out of the window as virtual reality steps in.

FLEXIBLE FULFILLMENT OPTIONS

A speedy and smooth delivery process is part of the customer's shopping experience, and retailers will have to go above and beyond to make order fulfillment a short wait. Retailers are already moving from having one mode of delivery to offering several different options to make it convenient for everyone. Whether a customer is in a hurry to receive the parcel or not, there is a mode of delivery waiting for you. Customers want speed and convenience when it comes to picking or ordering their parcels, and in this regard, retailers will have to provide unique options to align their payment and delivery systems.

ON-DEMAND CUSTOMER SERVICE

It can be difficult for a customer to find a store associate who can guide them to the right product or fetch it for them. The future of retail calls for on-demand customer services leveraging mobile applications, which will help the retailers maximize their staff, and enhance the customer experience. Shoppers will be able to request virtual assistance when and where they need it, inside the store.

Through tablet devices, the service associate can instantly find out about the customer's shopping preferences and history to provide a suggestion for an efficient buying experience. This is called predictive analysis and retailers will use it to find out what customers want before they even ask for it, or possibly before they even know they want it.

EASIER PAYMENT OPTIONS

Along with delivery modes, payment options are also going to become more convenient as retailers tap into the technology of Easy Pay and the likes, which promote self-mobile checkout. No shopper likes to wait in line to check out, and this could be a powerful magnet draw to consumers who can scan their products, choose their payment mode, and finalize their transaction without having to wait in line or for someone to process their order. This will, however, require the customer's trust in contactless payment but it will enable them to decide when and where to checkout, providing more convenience.

SOCIAL MEDIA

Social media has already changed a lot for retailers, but it will further change out communication and interactions. The aim of retailers will lie on building trust and relationships through their websites and not selling products. Retailers have to become leaders, not followers and actively participate in community forums to show interest as well as gauge the interest of their target market, know what they are saying and respond to problems as they are complaining.

Be it any retail business that you own, having a social media presence is important as well as maintaining that presence. Just having a website won't cut it any longer for retailers who want to set themselves apart and rise above the competition. With one click, retailers can convert their browsers into shoppers and show them recommendations as they learn more about their customer's tastes and preferences. Social media tools can help conduct surveys and gauge responses, which can help retailers, align their business strategy accordingly.

Smart devices are already making their mark in helping customers entertain their every whim. However, in spite of that, the Internet of Things is still slow in its penetration with around 87% of customers still not having any idea of the term. Services like Google Now and Amazon's Dash Button are reshaping how customers interact and opt for their shopping, but for retailers, this could be one of the changes that will slowly and steadily make its way to adoption. If the Internet of Things takes over, it could radically change how retailers understand and respond to their logistics and demand and supply needs as it will increasingly help to refine and fine tune the processes in the best way possible.

What has really changed, and will further change in the future, is how customers interact with retailers. Technology has already put a lot of power in the customer's hand and mind, and now, no amount of brainwashing makes an impact on the customer unless they really want to buy a product themselves. Customers have access to increased information in the palm of their hands, which allows them to find and read product reviews, post their own reviews, and fish for information. They have become capable of making their own decisions, and while retailers can influence their customers in a way, they can't make their decision for them any longer.

No retailer has the power to tell the customer that they should buy a certain product unless of course, they have developed that level of trust with them. For retailers to reach that level with their customers, they will have to work on building trust and relationships, which changes the whole game. Power has been shifted to the consumer, and the retailer needs to think of their customer more than the business.

If you do not value your customer today, you will lose them and probably some others, as word of mouth marketing has made a strong foothold. People tend to follow what other people tell them as opposed to retailers or brands because of increased transparency. Businesses are becoming transparent for their customers so that they know exactly what they are choosing. Businesses are helping customers make the right choice in this way, which shows how far retailers have come from dictating their products to customers to allowing them the choice to make their own decision.

Today and in the future, retailers are walking on a thin line of trust, which if broken, will lead to a significant loss. This loss will result in not only dipped profits but also abandoned customers and the possible loss of not just one customer with whom you had severed your ties but others as well because social media plays a prominent role in spreading the word.

The shift in power to the consumer means that business is walking a tightrope and needs to think about their every action very carefully. The future calls for the use of technology in enhancing the customer experience and making it as convenient as possible. Retail giants like Amazon are using drone technology to deliver their parcels more efficiently and quickly which essentially means they are thinking about making the delivery process more convenient for their customers.

They are eliminating wait time. Be it a brick and mortar store or an online retail site or any other kind of retail business, how you can enhance your customer's experience is what will matter in the future.

THE LAST WORD

It is not easy for retailers to boost sales and profits in a competitive environment, but they can certainly do so quickly by paying close attention to the gaps and addressing external and internal factors. If you think that there are too many factors causing hindrance to growth in sales, start by identifying and correcting internal gaps.

Usually, it is never just one factor that causes a business to suffer, in my experience; it is generally a combination of many "mini" issues that causes the decline. What I outlined here may address most of the common issues, but if you are facing some serious problems, it is time for you to analyze everything from A to Z and try to identify and note down each and every issue. Then start one by one and try to solve them. Don't try to solve all at once, instead, start with the smallest issue and work your way up to the bigger ones.

Now as for sales and marketing, I do believe a smart marketing strategy mixed with great merchandising and awesome pricing strategy can take most retail businesses to the next level especially when you can trust your employees and know that they are loyal.

Motivated and committed employees automatically contribute to the growth of the company because they become influencers themselves. Customers today look for a positive experience with a retailer to progress their relationship with them, and if you fall behind in providing that experience to your customers, then you fall behind in boosting your profits.

Once a retailer has a strong team of committed employees to work with, which helps them to grow, then you can start using the external influence to enhance brand awareness, communication, and customer relationships. Retailers, who are successful in maintaining a positive social image, engage with customers, respond to their queries, and make the shopping experience easier for them, are more likely to drive their sales.

It is vital for retailers to understand the changing consumer dynamics and act accordingly. If you don't use the right techniques and tools to reach your audience, it is unlikely that you will gain positive results. However, if you can deploy the best tactics to attract customers both online and offline, it can go a long way in helping you to boost your sales.

Remember, that your customer has considerable power today because of the plethora of choices available, and if you are not going to reach out to them personally or extend a hand of friendship, the consumer will not bother to do business with you. Retailers have little influence over customers, but the way you gain that influence has changed.

It is time to change and understand your consumer on a deeper level to drive sales and reap positive results and profits.

I hope you enjoyed reading my work, once again I am not a professional writer, so my sincere apology in advance in case you find any typos or errors in my book.

Feel free to contact me for any additional information or help you may need; I will be happy to help you. Thanks and Good Luck!!!

www.ingramcontent.com/pod-product-compliance
Lightning Source LLC
Chambersburg PA
CBHW071818200526
45169CB00018B/389